Contents

Introduction

Friday evening. Throughout Britain climbers are packing rucksacks and making rendezvous. Soon they will begin to travel towards the hills and coastlines. It doesn't matter how: by coach, minibus, train, motorcycle, battered van or family saloon. Tonight they will erect tents by torchlight, unlock the doors of club huts, unroll sleeping bags in disused cowsheds, or book into hotels. Some will be teenagers; most will be in their early twenties; many will be approaching middle age; while a few will be closer to sixty or seventy. Men and women: students, engineers, factory workers, secretaries, teachers, shop assistants, doctors. Nothing identifies them as rock climbers but their common purpose this Friday night.

Later the talk will be of success and failure on the crags the previous weekend, or of ambitions for the coming season. A tale of outrageous behaviour will receive its hundredth telling, becoming a little more colourful and a lot less truthful on its way into myth and legend. Eventually plans for tomorrow will be developed, each a little too ambitious but fuelled into the realms of possibility by the atmosphere of daring which prevails.

Saturday brings rain, hangovers and paralysing doubts. The morning light floods the valleys only to be sucked into the shadows of the cliffs. Already the cloud begins to curl down from the summits, brushing the rocks with a slippery coat of moisture. The warm glow of anticipation evaporates to leave only the cold gnawing of trepidation.

Rucksacks are heavy, the approach tedious. Muffled shouts fall to earth and betray the presence of others already at work high on the cliff. For a few seconds the mists part to reveal a bizarre mannequin swathed in coloured loops and shining metal, jigging uncertainly from foot to foot and moaning softly. His partner, meanwhile, linked by the rope, hides his pale face inside a cave to fend off vertigo. From time to time they call to each other, as if to relieve the overwhelming sense of loneliness which grips them. The echoes mingle half-way until taken by the wind. The mists close again and they are gone.

Down below things are going no better; some equipment has been forgotten, the rope lies in a tangle. Muttered recriminations threaten to divide the partnership before the climb has properly begun.

The mood changes with the first movements, as if the touch and texture of rock trigger a well-practised routine which has the power to stem the rising tide of uncertainty. This is it. Your body responds by leaning, pulling and pushing in harmony. The process has become an elevated dance, the cliff its tilted stage. Curtains of rock hang to each side as you creep skyward, the rope trailing behind as an anchor on life and reality.

Rhythm and movement falter where the rock begins to bulge out above your head. The fingers of your left hand mechanically curl over a small flake of rock, while your body hangs vertically beneath like a sack suspended from a hook. Meanwhile, the fingers of your right hand begin burrowing into a crack. The knuckles, red with abrasion, bleed gently from a raised flap of skin; but there is no pain and the injury seems unimportant. To ease the strain your legs spread themselves wide, bridging across the opposing walls of the corner. The right leg vibrates with fatigue and threatens to dislodge your foot from its hold. Strength is fading; the next five seconds will be crucial.

The fingers finally lock into the crack. Relief surges through your body. The left arm screams for release, but instead you wrench up on it, kicking free from the puzzle that has pinned you to that one place for so long. A hidden strength peels back the blanket of anxiety; your limbs pull and press together, choreographed by a brain turned hyperactive through adrenalin. The dance resumes, fuelled by gasps of upwelling air.

Exhilaration subsides at the top of the climb while you concentrate on belaying the rope to safeguard your partner's ascent. Soon a feeling of weariness will smother the lingering glow of satisfaction. In silence you will coil the ropes and begin the easy scramble to regain the foot of the cliff, but by then your thoughts will be turning to the next climb and the new problems it will bring. Rock climbing is an addictive drug, and once is not enough.

First movements on rock are often scrambling ones, encountered perhaps while following one of the famous ridge walks. This common ground blurs any theoretical line of demarcation drawn between walking and climbing, so that only when pursued at their extremes do the two experiences appear unrelated.

Having been inspired by early scrambling experiences to take up 'proper' rock climbing, it would be a mistake to delve immediately into the technicalities of ropework. Ropes can interfere badly with the exhilaration of moving unaided and unfettered over steep rock. It is much better to find some local outcrop or quarry and simply climb around its base. The absence of danger will help you shed a debilitating tenseness which often afflicts those first hesitant movements. If one section proves too difficult, simply jump off and start somewhere else – you won't be letting anyone down and you won't feel under pressure to perform.

Bouldering, as this entertaining branch of climbing is known, can be a rewarding pursuit in itself, but there is more to rock climbing than problem solving and athletic movement. What would it be like, you wonder, to be threading a route up one of the really big crags? Here the sort of problems encountered on small outcrops are piled one above the other in a vertical maze – some obvious and challenging, others concealed and lurking – while the proximity of danger adds spice to the adventure.

Such is the nature of the sport that even a mildly ambitious climber will sometimes attempt routes that are a fraction too difficult. On such occasions the risk of falling – always present to some degree – multiplies alarmingly. To combat this, elaborate protection methods are employed. Not that rock climbing can ever be thought completely safe – it never is. In fact, sophistication of rope technique is deliberately suppressed in order to confine the equipment to its passive role as a safety net. This preserves the essential nature of the sport so that no amount of ropes and hardware will get you up a difficult climb if your body or spirit is lacking.

You will soon discover that the cliff you aspire to climb – you might have passed below it during a hill walk or seen a photograph in a book on mountains – has been climbed before. In fact, a dozen or more routes will probably have been pioneered up its various facets, the most interesting of them being repeated four or five times every fine weekend. These routes will have names, and their lefts and rights will be meticulously described in a guidebook which you can buy from the local equipment shop. Inevitably, some of the mystery evaporates with this discovery. In compensation the guidebook will reveal a hundred-year-old history of rock climbing which surrounds the cliffs and climbs with intrigue and renown.

1 Rock

Few sports insist on such intimate contact with the medium as does rock climbing. Skis intervene between skier and snow, the canoe between canoeist and water. In rock climbing that searching and gripping with bare fingers is unique. Despite modern terminology, this is manifestly a primitive action; something a wild animal might do, with its animal fears, strengths and daring.

Your first encounter with rock may ultimately prove to be the most significant. It has the power to shape your whole attitude towards the sport. I know that mine did. I was fifteen years old and struggling miserably with the knots of adolescence. School was a particular problem. Early academic promise had failed to materialise, while my athletic prowess – never astounding at the best of times (a cheerless fourteenth in the annual cross-country) – was fast crumbling in the face of youthful indolence and assorted bad habits. My life lacked direction.

Absenting myself from classes for a few days, I hitched two hundred miles to visit my sister in South Wales – a perilous journey for one so innocent. She was studying at Swansea University, and I landed on her doorstep in the week preceding final examinations. However, she took me in with great kindness and understanding, none of which I appreciated at the time. I passed several important milestones during the brief period of my stay, although at the time I was unaware that between them they would stake out the perimeter of my future. The most significant event was that I was taken rock climbing.

A visit to the Gower coast with the college climbing club had been promised from the outset. It was an exciting proposition, although I knew nothing of what to expect. True I had done some fell walking in the Lake District, but oddly enough had no recollection of the cliffs and climbers I must have seen. What had impressed me more were the stories Jenny told about her climbing adventures. I was very proud of her and doubted that anyone else in the country – let alone the school – could boast a sister who had once fallen down a crevasse in an Alpine glacier. What troubled my mind as we caught the bus out of town was the tenuous link between the Alps and the Three Cliffs. Was it really possible that somewhere on a nearby beach, mixed up with bikinis and ice-creams, there would be cliffs worthy of the attention of real climbers? I feared a deception, but went along anyway.

The cliffs were real enough. As we rounded the headland three huge fins of rock came into view, rising from the sands as if some great prehistoric beast lay buried there. A tremendous feeling of excitement welled up inside me. I wanted to rush across to the rocks and begin climbing at once, except that I did not know how to climb. Instead, I laced up my corduroy beach shoes, feigned indifference and waited patiently for the adventure to begin.

The club had enough rope for just two groups of climbers, and those places had already been claimed. Some of those who had tied on appeared unwilling to start and were obviously inventing excuses for the delay – fiddling with knots, cleaning boot soles, arranging equipment. This seemed a terrible injustice when set against my own eagerness.

I was choking with frustration. Jenny clearly understood my condition (or had seen an opportunity to rid herself of a pesky brother) and proposed that we should climb unroped. I agreed at once. She urged me to follow her movements precisely, to test each handhold carefully and, above all, not to fall off. Then we began.

At first we moved easily over sea-scoured lower rocks, Jenny climbing nimbly in bare feet despite flesh ripping encrustations of shells. Soon the cliff reared up into a wall of bubbly rock. So futile did the direct attempt appear that I guessed we would find an easy way around, but Jenny moved on to the steeper rock without a pause, her hands and feet moving over its surface without hesitation. My trust in her was total; I also moved on to the steepening face.

By now the tide had turned and the first tongues of water were licking the lowest rocks. The sound of cheerful banter passing between the other climbers drowned in the waves which thumped and sloshed through the natural arch in the cliff base. I doubted the possibility of retreat. 'Don't look down,' Jenny said. But, gripped by curiosity, I *did* look down: down beyond shoes half supported on a narrow ledge; down beyond folds of rock already climbed. I expected to be frightened, but instead was exhilarated. To be poised between earth and sky – neither moving nor staying, secure nor falling – seemed to me to be the most wonderful sensation imaginable.

Whenever I moved, patches of rock would, in turn, enlarge in vision and snap into sharp focus. If one contained no usable hold, it would blur and shrink back into the mass while another was selected and searched. If this new patch revealed a hold, a hand would dart up and settle there, its fingers nestling into the indentations. At some synchronised signal the body would tighten and lean, a foot extending across the wall to maintain balance.

With each move made, another search would begin. I wished it would go on for ever.

Quite suddenly I realised that we had climbed to within a few metres of the summit. With the goal now in sight I only wanted it all to be over, to sit exultant on the topmost rock and look down on people small as ants scurrying from the incoming tide, to pity them for their lowly situation. Although the climbing had become much easier, some of the holds rattled alarmingly in their sockets like rotten teeth. I knew I must be very careful not to rush and make a mistake. How ironic that would be! Muscles tensed so that I began to move in jerks like a teetering wooden doll, lunging for holds and committing my weight to them without prior test. A vision flashed through my mind of a body surging in and out of the sea arch on a rising tide…

My recollection ends there. Oddly enough I cannot remember reaching the top – my first real summit – although we must have passed over it in order to reach safety on the grass slopes beyond. Our arrival on top must have seemed an anticlimax after the experiences below.

I am not suggesting that my own initiation to rock climbing was in any way typical or laudable, but I count myself fortunate in being able to look back on it with such profound happiness. I have never relinquished or renounced the sensations I experienced on my first climb, however naive they might seem in retrospect. In fact, I suspect I have been subconsciously trying to recreate them in all my subsequent adventures, and to this day I take special delight in climbing unroped.

Your first experience of climbing will certainly be very different from mine, but I sincerely hope that it will engage the true spirit of the sport in some way. If you have yet to touch rock I would urge you to make that first encounter in the company of friends, relatives, or club acquaintances – even if later you choose to learn the rudiments of ropework with a paid instructor. This first 'climb' need not be a recognised route; it could be a steep rise in a gully scramble, or a toppled boulder below cliffs. What matters is that you make the effort of your own volition, not through a sense of duty when fifth in line at the end of an instructor's rope.

This story has an epilogue. A few years ago I returned to the Gower in the hope of rediscovering my roots. I suppose I ought to have known better. The Three Cliffs, now appearing as unimpressive lumps in the sand, did not seem at all familiar. Holiday-makers lounged in beach chairs at their foot while I scrambled up and down the rocks trying, unsuccessfully as it turned out, to find some feature that would remind me of where I had gone all those years before. While searching, I was distracted by an impressively smooth slab of rock which cut across the roof of a natural arch. It would make an excellent climb.

The rock was steep right from the start and after a few upward moves I thought about going down. But something took hold of me and I found myself going on – reaching, pulling, swaying – until before long I stepped on to some tiny footholds above the arch itself. On this occasion it was low water, so the tide which surged through the tunnel beneath was one of people. Some of them paused to look up at me for a few seconds, surprised or curious, before continuing to where they had left towels and suntan lotion. For a moment I felt

---

IN SUMMARY

• Rock climbing is the purest of adventure sports in that progress – unlike in skiing or canoeing – relies on hands and feet alone.

• Even those with little conventional sporting ability can excel at rock climbing.

• Your first experience of rock climbing may occur during a hill walk, while exploring fallen boulders below a cliff, during a stay at an outdoor centre, or on the climbing wall at the local sports centre.

• Your first experience of rock climbing may shape your entire future climbing aspirations.

• Climbing with paid instructors, though relatively safe, does not represent the true essence of the sport.

• Both beginner and expert are playing the same game; what separates them is subtlety of technique.

• Rock climbing has an addictive quality.

---

ridiculous perched up there above their heads, clinging to a lump of rock and a fading memory, but the climb had become an absorbing one and in need of all my concentration if I was to succeed. Locking my fingertips into the creases, I kicked up with taut muscles towards the summit. The movement rekindled an old memory. I wished it would go on forever.

2 First Climbs

What a difference the rope makes! It shows that you mean business, that you have outgrown 'mere' scrambling and now seek real trouble (don't worry – you'll find it). Of course, this new status bars you from further fraternisation with non-climbers; not that you would find anything they had to say to be of the slightest interest. Instead you should remain silent and aloof and adopt the grim expression of a mountaineer closing with his fate…

It was my first telegram: 'Meet M6/A5 Friday 9p.m. for Wales', it said, 'Bring boots and butties. Tony.' I felt very important. This was the long-awaited summons from my brother. He had a rope; this would be the real thing. I searched the hall cupboard for a pair of hiking boots that might pass for proper climbing boots – hard luck if they happened to be three sizes too big.

Our lifts from opposite ends of the country dropped us at a windswept Cannock Chase within five minutes of each other. Tony wore his army combat gear; I made do with my school anorak and mountaineer's expression. We travelled to Wales together and asked our driver to put us down on the crest of a bleak pass. Rain lashed against the windscreen. All we could see in the headlights were stone walls and a fallen telephone line thrashing in the wind. We watched the rear lights blur and disappear into the night before turning down the farm track.

Voiceless stares shone back at us in the torch beam as we flung open the barn door. In each straw-filled pit nestled a pair of climbers, cosy in their sleeping bags. No vacancies. We found a thinly padded shelf and wrapped ourselves up, wet and shivering, in our blankets. I fell asleep listening to the scratching of rats among the rafters.

We awoke to the drumming of rain on the roof tiles. An enticing aroma penetrated the blankets – fried bacon. Peering down, we watched the early risers hunched goblin-like over roaring paraffin stoves. For some reason they appeared in no rush to leave. We pulled on boots, ate half our stock of beef paste sandwiches, and set off for the hills.

A film of water rippled over the rock, bloating pads of lichen into slippery sponges. Rain soaked our clothes until they hung from our shoulders like wash rags. My fingers had turned white with cold. Tony pointed to a sinister groove; probably the drainage downpipe for that part of the crag. A small waterfall issued from its base. 'We'll climb that,' he said, arranging the rope around my waist and hands in the prescribed manner. He kicked each boot against the rock to dislodge mud from the soles and then set off up the groove in optimistic mood. I thought it all very exciting.

At first Tony made reasonable progress by pulling himself up on small spikes of rock and resting between times by wedging himself in the angle of the groove. The spikes got smaller and smaller until, at about housetop height, they disappeared altogether. Now he was reduced to a sort of fast pedalling motion with his feet. I assumed this to be an accepted technique on these harder climbs. Evidently I was wrong. To his credit he kept his dignity to the last and let go without a squeak, but events were beyond his control after that and he rumbled down the groove towards me like a sack in a coal chute. The rope hung limp in my arms; obviously I could do nothing to help him so instead I sought to help myself. I jumped aside at the last moment, leaving his way clear to fetch up spread-eagled over a boulder at my feet. He emitted a long, low groan. I assumed this sort of thing often happened so tried not to make a fuss. Fortunately Tony was merely winded and was soon on his feet again. He made a spirited attempt to re-enter the groove, having read somewhere that a fallen leader risked losing his nerve unless he immediately re-addressed the rock. However, I pointed out that the climb was probably beyond me and he graciously agreed to postpone the attempt. We retreated to the barn for a second breakfast of beef paste.

Among other things, this first experience of roped climbing taught us that we could not fall off with impunity. I suppose our youthful exuberance had got the better of us. In fact, we had made not one but several mistakes: poor choice of route, misuse of equipment, ignorance of conditions, wrong assessment of difficulties and inadequate preparation. Heaven help us had we got any higher up the cliff. I would not wish this traumatic experience on any beginner, and yet we must all learn from our mistakes. What I would suggest is that you use other people's mistakes to learn from – it is much less painful. Ideally, you should at least try to understand the fundamentals of rope protection, its applications and limitations, before you reach neck-breaking height on a big cliff. Later chapters have the details.

Finding someone to take you climbing may not be easy. Unless someone is known to you personally, your best alternative might be to join a local climbing club. Magazines listed in the bibliography include the addresses of club secretaries. Additionally some schools and

Fig 1 A typical first climb: large holds, frequent ledges and not too steep (Pulpit route (D), Milestone Buttress, North Wales).

most colleges will support clubs of their own, often with an equipment pool of specialised items such as ropes, helmets and harnesses. Joining a club has advantages beyond those of securing partners, borrowing equipment and sharing transport costs. Most importantly of all, you will make lasting friendships with people who share your enthusiasm for climbing.

A second alternative is to enrol on a climbing course organised by an outdoor activities centre or qualified guide. You will receive expert tuition on ropework and might find yourself climbing difficult routes by the end of the week. For all that, however, the professional environment is an unnatural one and certainly no long-term substitute for regular climbing partners.

I have to admit that I never joined a club or went on a climbing course when I began climbing (although I have since been associated with both in various capacities). Instead, having survived our violent encounter with the water-washed groove, my brother and I taught ourselves the basic techniques which we then applied with great caution. As a consequence, our progress up the ladder of difficulty was very slow indeed; some five years elapsed before we felt ready to lead *Extreme* grade routes, and we never did climb the hardest routes of the day. There are no regrets, though, because we have had the satisfaction of making each new discovery for ourselves.

It could be that your first climb takes place on a small outcrop no more than ten metres

Fig 2 Young people attending an Outdoor Centre climbing course.

high, in which case it will not be necessary to regroup on midway ledges as you would on a bigger cliff. Instead, the leader will climb straight to the top in one go. Ropework will be straightforward and there will be few communication problems. In fact, you can still climb even if no one is willing or capable of leading. What happens is that someone will gain the top of the climb by finding an easy scramble to one side. He will then lower down the rope end for each climber to tie on and ascend in turn. The method is called *top roping* and allows all members of the party to receive the full protection of the rope. It is particularly useful when climbing on unreliable rock, such as soft sandstone. However, top roping is not generally used in other circumstances because it bypasses the uncertainty of the lead – an intangible and possibly romantic concept which lies at the heart of the sport's tradition.

Everyone begins by seconding, only later progressing to sharing the lead. The role of the second is a vital one, since without proper rope handling and moral support even the most able leader cannot function. This is why all roped climbs are undertaken as partnerships, although this is something you may not appreciate at first. Eventually you will come to realise that it is the whole enterprise which is important, not just a daring individual lead. So never consider yourself a passenger in a climb, however expert your companions. Enjoyment of both the climb and the day will depend on you as much as anyone else.

Tony and I attempted our first 'big' climb twelve months after that first outing. That night in the barn (the same one, although we now had the luxury of stove, food and sleeping bags) we agonised over the decision for hours. Grooved Arete was a famous classic climb on the 250m high East Face of Tryfan – a wonderful rocky peak dominating the Ogwen Valley in Snowdonia. It would be our

I could not get to sleep that night. What if we met impossible difficulties high on the cliff, perhaps on the Knight's Slab which the guide-book had described in such sinister terms? If I slipped from its diagonal traverse I might swing beyond help into unknown grooves. The whole prospect filled me with an unset-tling mixture of longing and trepidation. Eventually I fell asleep exhausted with anxiety.

We awoke to a fine summer's day, the morning rays falling obliquely on the moun-tain so that even at this distance we could pick out the line of our route.

All Tryfan's East Face climbs begin from a terrace which slants across the face – that would be our first objective. We followed a narrow path which zigzagged up a heather

Fig 3 Acrobatic climbing on Flake Climb (S) at Ilkley, a gritstone outcrop in Yorkshire.

Fig 4 The crux of Murray's Route (S) on Dow Crag, a popular mountain crag in the Lake District.

most difficult climb to date. This time we were better prepared. Our equipment, although still fairly primitive, was at least adequate, and we were more fully aware of its potential and limitations. More importantly, we had bought a guidebook which told us the location of good climbs and how difficult we might expect them to be. On the traditional and somewhat archaic grading scale (still in use), Grooved Arete rated *Hard Very Difficult*. In everyday climbing parlance this translates as 'fairly easy', although as comparative begin-ners we were certain to be taxed to our limit.

slope and entered a stone-filled runnel. Impatient for the real climbing, we rushed straight up a tongue of unstable rocks thinking it to be the path. In fact, it was a scree run used only in descent. We wasted a great deal of energy on it.

The terrace itself is a remarkable feature; you might mistake it for an ancient trackway cut across the mountainside. We joined a straggling caravan which was already making its way along. In front and behind, small groups of people toiled against the slope and the hot sun. At intervals they would cast off their burden of rope and rucksack and fling themselves down in a panting heap at the foot of their chosen climb, making a great show of being glad to have the walking part over and done with. We did likewise at the foot of Grooved Arete, allowing ourselves a slightly superior smirk because it happened to be one of the harder climbs. Ours was none the less a popular climb, so Tony insisted we sat at its very foot to prevent late comers from sneaking in before us.

Tony placed a sling over a flake of rock while I uncoiled the rope. This anchor would secure me to the rock while I belayed. Nervous but excited, I paid out rope a few centimetres at a time while Tony worked his way up the first awkward fissure. Twenty metres higher he gained a room-sized ledge, passed a sling over the top of a large block and secured himself to it with a length of rope. Now that Tony was secure I released the belay so he could pull in the spare rope between us. A few moments later it tightened at my waist – no going back now. I was eager to start but had to wait until he called for me to climb before removing by own anchor sling and making ready to begin.

Once I had started climbing I forgot about the increasing drop below my feet and concentrated on making the best use of holds. Tony had shouted down a few suggestions,

but it was pointless trying to remember precisely which holds he had used. Instead I worked out each problem for myself, safeguarded throughout by the rope which Tony drew in – neither tight nor slack – to match my every upward move. Our reunion at the ledge jolted us from private reveries.

We encountered our first real trial at the twin grooves. The guidebook had warned us to expect some precarious climbing, but Tony was still surprised by the smoothness of it all. From my stance below and to one side I could see little of what was happening, but could judge by erratic rope movements and an occasional grunt that the climbing was difficult. Moments later Tony bobbed into view, quite high now, with a wild look in his eye. He appeared to be searching for something and twitched with rodent-like urgency. The fact

Fig 5 Problem solving on Merlin, a Tremadog VS.

that a slip would result in a twenty-metre fall on to broken rocks might have had something to do with it. Eventually he found what he was looking for – protection. With some strain he held on with one hand while threading a sling through a small hole in the rock; there was a good deal of swearing before he succeeded. Joining the two ends of the sling together with a karabiner, he clipped in his rope and let out a great sigh of relief. So did I. Provided the sling held firm, a slip now would result in a fall of only a few metres – twice the distance he happened to be above this 'runner' at the time. With this reassurance he completed the pitch without further hesitation.

When my turn came to follow I feared I might need a pull on the rope to help me over the difficult part. Instead I was surprised to find the groove quite straightforward and I reached Tony's threaded sling without difficulty. I removed the sling, placed it over my shoulders and proceeded up what I thought would be an easy finish. How wrong I was! I landed on the ledge with a gasp, much to Tony's amusement, and acknowledged his good lead of the pitch.

The slender 'grooved arete' itself rose above us now in a single majestic sweep, knifing into the huge black tower which dominated this part of the face. Unknown difficulties lay ahead; we could not relax. We ate lunch and looked down on some tiny figures, rucksacks bobbing on their backs, as they inched their way up the terrace in the full heat of the afternoon sun. We were in shade and, at an altitude of 800m, conscious of a cold edge to the wind. By now the valley bottom was so far below us that it no longer seemed part of this chaotic world of rock.

The grooved arete surrendered without a struggle – apart from one occasion when it tricked Tony into going too high. Misled by an ambiguity in the guidebook description, he was forced to reverse down a few metres

IN SUMMARY

Rope Security
• You can risk learning the art of climbing movement by trial and error, but not the science of rope technique.
• Climbing with ropes does not automatically confer safety. In some cases, the rope will at best reduce the severity of injuries.
• A climbing course is a good way to learn the basics of rope technique (*see* Appendix).

Finding Climbs and Climbing Partners
• The many thousands of established rock climbs are described in detail in pocket-sized guidebooks.
• Finding regular climbing partners is not easy at first; consider joining a local club (*see* Appendix for address sources). School and college clubs also generally keep pools of equipment.

Building Experience
• Begin by seconding climbs; don't attempt to lead until you have gained more experience in rope technique.
• The second, nevertheless, plays an important role in the climbing partnership.
• Top-roping on small outcrops is one way for an inexperienced partnership to develop skills in relative safety.

The Mind Game
• Climbing on big mountain crags is a complete experience, with the huge setting and uncertainties about weather and route-finding adding to the adventure.
• All climbers must endure moments of great anxiety; learning mental control is at least as important as developing pure technical ability.

(always harder than going up) until he could rejoin the correct route leading to the Haven.

For some reason I felt deeply anxious at the Haven. Here we were, I thought, trapped on some God-forsaken ledge in the middle of a huge cliff, probably unable to retreat down the last pitch and unlikely to get up the next, the notorious Knight's Slab. Historical notes in the guidebook told of a fatality here: imagine some poor climber slithering from his holds and plunging into the abyss. We should never have attempted the stupid climb; was it really worth it? I vowed that I would never go climbing again.

Such is the power of imagination and reputation. In fact, we climbed the Knight's Slab without undue difficulty. It was a relief to discover that it possessed any holds at all. Tony grinned down at me as I discovered for myself the key sequence which led intricately but securely up and across the chessboard slab.

This stance was tiny in comparison to all preceding ones – no bigger than a hall table. Engrossed in safely swapping anchors we had failed to notice the cloud now swirling around us, threatening damp and drizzle. If we had felt apprehensive at the Haven, we ought now to have felt terrified on this perch so dramatically set above an awesome drop. It induced precisely the opposite feeling – we had nothing to lose. Our confidence in each other was absolute. Nothing was going to stop us now; neither the cloud nor the rain nor the slippery rocks, not even the evil looking corner which rose above our heads and promised a grim struggle. The rope buzzed with the power and the certainty of what we were doing.

Nothing did stop us. Before long we had coiled the rope above the final pitch and had begun scrambling up easy rocks to the summit. I was filled with an indescribable joy. It had not been easy, but nowhere had we climbed recklessly. We had crossed a major threshold in our climbing careers.

3   Leading

Enthusiastic beginners usually aspire to share the lead on their climbs. The reasons for this are diverse, ranging from simple curiosity through to visions of death or glory. Whatever the motivation, there is no doubt that leading adds depth to the climbing experience.

My own chance to lead came six months after our graduation on Grooved Arete. Ogwen, our usual haunt, would have welcomed us gladly, but as climbers of ambition we felt obliged to seek out grim surroundings to match our grim expressions. The Llanberis Pass was in gloomy mood that bleak December day as we negotiated its bends on my over laden motorcycle. At either side a scree littered hillside swept down at an ugly angle to meet its opposing slope in the sunless V of the valley base. Small cliffs studded the northern slope, their vertical faces gathering up a few scraps of winter sunlight. Among them was Carreg Wastad, an unusually compact crag rippled by apparently unstable flutings. We stopped to admire its central feature, a jutting prow undercut by a band of overhangs. This was Crackstone Rib, our number one objective in the Pass. Neither of us had actually seen the route before, although we had been exposed to so many photographic evocations of the climb (silhouettes being the preferred treatment) that this made no difference.

The cliff was deserted, gripped by cold – just like us. We uncoiled the rope in silence. Tony handed me a rope end: 'Your lead,' he said, ignoring my gasp of astonishment. Evidently he had planned this for me all along.

The climbing began with a runnel polished smooth by the passage of thousands of boot soles. Down it trickled a vein of water, spoiling what little remained of foot friction. Self-confidence ebbed away. Tony waited patiently a few metres below while I discovered the problems of fixing runners. Eventually I succeeded in lodging one of our few nut runners in the crack and resumed the ascent with renewed courage. Unfortunately my boot caught in the sling as I stepped up. The nut rattled down the rope on its karabiner and slid into Tony's waiting hand. Furious at my incompetence I flung myself at the rock, heaving and pulling on holds which might easily have given way under my weight. It was a reckless performance.

Momentum carried me on to a steeper face, but in my haste I had failed to notice the rock spike at its foot which would have taken a reliable sling runner. Now I was stuck. I rapidly became frightened as I clung to my small finger holds and wondered what to do next. I searched for somewhere to place a runner, but could find no crack or flake in the compact rock. Jagged rocks waited below. Leading was no fun after all, I decided.

Slowly, I began to climb back down the wall. Tony offered encouragement and pointed out holds as best he could, but really it was a personal struggle. Although I was terrified and on the brink of panic, my limbs seemed to be doing all the right things. A flood of relief swept over me when finally I stepped down on to a ledge below the wall. Back in control, I placed a sling over the spike and clipped in the rope. Tony looked worried – as well he might – and asked if I was prepared to continue. However, with the runner fixed I felt much happier and nodded my intentions;

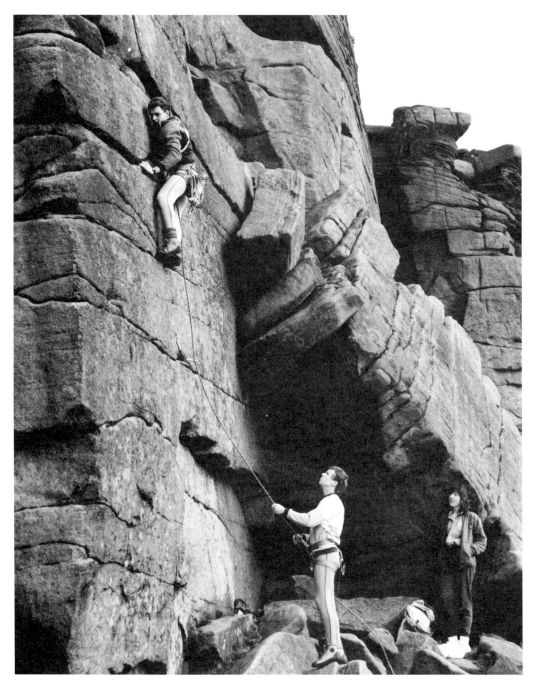

Fig 6 Leading demands confidence in yourself and trust in your second. Heather Wall, a Hard Severe on Stanage Edge.

with its protection the traverse seemed effortless. A few minutes later I arrived at a tiny ledge adjacent to the rib.

While self-consciously mumbling the unfamiliar leader's calls I anchored to a cluster of spikes, drew in the slack rope and made ready to belay. Secretly I hoped someone might pass below the crag and look up wondering who this bold and capable leader at work on Crackstone Rib might be. But only Tony saw me, and he was not so easily impressed. All the same, it was thrilling to trace the arc of rope where it crossed the wall below and marvel at the fact that I had climbed up there protected by nothing more than a crotchety spike.

Tony brought me down to earth. With his fist he thumped the anchor spikes to demonstrate their looseness. Then he complained that the securing loop was too slack. Finally he criticised my choice of body position, implying that had he fallen I would have been pulled off my feet, probably letting go of the rope. My pride was dented. Why was he trying to spoil everything? 'But you didn't fall,' I protested. 'No, not this time,' was all he said. Of course, he was right. After putting everything in order he moved out on to the tiny holds of the rib and began climbing skywards, silhouetted by the afternoon sun. Just like the pictures.

The leader's role extends far beyond that of accepting the possibility of a longer fall. There are the extra responsibilities of route finding, of making stances secure, and of safeguarding the second during traverses. The rewards are also proportionately greater; not least that of being first to solve obstacles encountered on the route.

Fortunately, my supervised lead of Crackstone Rib exposed me to the immediate sensation and personal danger of leading without having to accept overall responsibility. Three months elapsed before I felt ready to lead a less experienced companion on a climb.

Fig 7 The traverse on Pedestal Route, a popular VDiff at the Roaches.

The decision making process began long before travelling to Wales. Dave had already agreed in principle to come climbing for the weekend, provided we would not be attempting anything too difficult. I needed to find a route which would prove exciting without taxing our limited experience. I borrowed some guidebooks to the area and began to study them closely.

I was tempted by some of the long climbs at Idwal and Lliwedd, but being early March we would risk encountering damp rock on their sunless faces. Besides, the air temperature at seven or eight hundred metres would be several degrees below what we might expect in the valleys. South facing cliffs at Tremadog promised an interesting day, but a glance through the guide revealed few good

Fig 8 Eliminate 'C', a VS on Dow Crag.

Fig 9 Lavaredo Wall, Carreg Alltrem. Large holds compensate for the verticality on this exposed VS.

climbs at a grade we might realistically attempt. Eventually I found what I was looking for – a climb called Flying Buttress on Dinas Cromlech in the Llanberis Pass. The cliff faced south, carried little drainage from the hillside above and could be reached from the road with a twenty-minute walk. Moreover, the guide described the route in glowing terms: 'a classic at the grade' (an amenable *Difficult*), it said, and awarded a maximum three stars for overall quality and interest. It had six pitches, none of them very long, promising plenty of variety. In the climb's 100m length there were ridges, pinnacles, exposed traverses, and – to keep us guessing to the end – an awkward chimney to finish.

The next day I approached Dave with the proposition, carefully playing down the difficulties mentioned in the guide – he was at a disadvantage since I contrived to leave the guidebook at home! Infected by my enthusiasm he agreed. I surreptitiously repossessed the guidebook and we left for Wales.

Dinas Cromlech towered above as we clattered up a slope of unstable scree. An open-book feature at its centre dominated our upward view whenever we paused for breath. This was Cenotaph Corner, the most famous climb in Britain. It looked holdless and impossibly steep; if someone had suggested then that I would climb it one day, I would have thought them insane. In comparison, the notched ridge of Flying Buttress which defined the right side of the crag, and towards which we now turned, looked to be little more than a scramble.

Dave seemed to be reluctant to anchor himself below the first pitch. He saw little point in it, he said, considering I could hardly fall further than the ground. I related an incident which took place the week before: a leader almost tugged from his holds by a restless second who had tripped over a boulder while wandering about at the foot of the crag. He took the point and fixed an anchor – one less worry.

The holds were large but polished, the climbing more difficult than we had been led to expect. Towards the end of the pitch the ridge steepened into a wall. Recalling the Crackstone Rib episode, I fixed a good runner before relinquishing my position of relative comfort on easier rocks. This would be my insurance if I failed to locate a runner on the wall itself. As a result I arrived on the first belay ledge still feeling in control. In his turn Dave climbed the pitch with ease, his long reach demolishing the few difficult moves. I suppressed a desire to see him struggle just a little.

The upper half of the ridge presented no major obstacles. I fixed a sling runner around one of the crenellations at its top and descended into the notch beyond. By now, however, the rope had passed between so many pinnacles that it was in danger of jamming. Even with two hands I could barely pull it through. Besides, I realised that Dave would not have the full protection of the rope while climbing down to join me in the notch. There was nothing for it but to climb back up to the crest and take my belay stance there.

Concerned by the delay Dave began calling up to me, but his words were muffled by the wind. Fearing a reply might be misinterpreted and lead to yet more confusion, I remained silent and concentrated instead on arranging the anchors. Once I had pulled up all the slack rope and arranged the belay, I gave three sharp tugs on the rope to indicate that he could begin climbing – our pre-arranged

signal if communication proved difficult. After his confirming reply of three tugs I felt the rope come slack as he began to climb. We were back in business. A few minutes later he passed by and 'led' the few metres down into the notch to occupy the next stance.

The mood changed. Having left behind the friendly ridge and its comforting holds we now contemplated the imposing walls of the upper buttress. A bitterly cold wind funnelled through the notch, further eroding our confidence. According to the guidebook the best climbing was yet to come, and I felt sure our spirits would rise once we got to grips with it, but Dave muttered something about 'giving it best' and pointed to what looked like an easy escape route on to scree at the side of the cliff. 'I'll just try the first few moves,' I said, 'and if it proves at all difficult I'll come back down.' Of course, I had not the slightest intention of coming down. 'It's all right,' I said, trying my best to make some awkward moves in a groove appear straightforward. Dave looked unconvinced but seemed resigned to his fate. The ruse had worked; we would go on.

An impressively situated traverse now led out leftwards to a ledge on the buttress front. Eager to reach it, I was tempted to begin the traverse at once, but then I realised that from my stance the rope would slant diagonally across to Dave while he tackled the difficult groove. Even a minor slip would develop into an appalling pendulum swing across the wall. If I placed a runner immediately above the groove, I reasoned, Dave would have the reassurance of rope protection from above. I placed the runner, clipped it to the rope and traversed easily across to the stance.

We felt vulnerable perched on our exposed ledge, with the wind gusting around us and unknown difficulties lurking above. With exaggerated care we exchanged positions so that Dave could belay my rope while I explored the next pitch. A few snowflakes

---

> ## IN SUMMARY
>
> *The Mentality of Leading*
> • Leading amplifies the climbing experience – both thrill and risk.
> • Self-confidence evaporates more quickly when leading.
> • Panic during early leads can result in either terrified immobility or reckless haste.
> • An apparently impossible sequence can prove straightforward once it has been protected.
>
> *Taking Care of your Second*
> • The leader generally chooses the climb and takes most of the route-finding decisions.
> • The leader is responsible for the complete safety of the second: arranging secure anchors at the belay ledges, placing protection specifically to minimise a pendulum swing, and so on.
> • When climbing with an inexperienced second, preserve communication and morale by reducing pitch lengths and arranging stances within visual contact.
>
> *Taking Care of Yourself*
> • Attempt your first leads under the supervision of an already experienced leader.
> • Always anchor inexperienced seconds at the foot of climbs to deter them from wandering about, tripping over and tugging you off the rock.
> • Think ahead. Anticipate difficulties and place protection before problems arise.
> • Arrange protection and belays in ways that avoid generating excessive rope drag.
> • Resist the urge to hurry when almost at the top; place some good final protection in case easy but dangerous ground awaits.

began to fall, brushing dryly against the cold rock. I feared for our morale and dared not mention them. I stepped up as if to begin but then faltered. What if I took the wrong route and climbed into yet greater difficulties? What if the snowfall worsened and began coating the footholds? What if…? I glanced down towards the boulder bed fifty metres below, but Dave's encouraging smile interrupted my line of sight. 'You'll be all right,' he said, motioning me to continue, the rope gripped firm in his hands.

As it happened, I had no choice but to follow the correct line. Smooth rock bulged above, forcing me to climb to the right across a slanting gangway. In ordinary circumstances the passage would have been simple, but my fingers were white with cold and I could no longer feel the texture of the rock. With agonising slowness I teetered across and clambered on to a broad ledge. For five minutes I crouched helpless, sobbing like a child from the pain of blood flowing back into my hands.

I guessed Dave would appreciate some moral support in return; instead of tying directly to the belay anchors – which would have placed me out of sight – I extended their securing loops so that I could stand overlooking the gangway. Finally I placed a subsidiary anchor immediately above to improve stability of the system. Now I could watch Dave's every move and offer encouragement should it become necessary.

'You didn't tell me about this,' Dave said, looking up at the chimney which barred us from the top. Dave hated chimneys, but the weather was getting worse and daylight had begun to fade – we had no option. I threw myself at the horrible fissure, determined to settle the issue one way or another. Almost at once my foot slipped and I slithered back on to the ledge. Dave said nothing. Our situation was fast becoming serious. I tried again, scrabbling with my knees, but it was no use and I flopped back down. Defeated by a *Diff*! The ignominy of it! Dave calmly pointed to a foothold which I had failed to notice in my haste. It was not much of a hold, but it would do. With its help I attained a tenable position in the chimney and wriggled up to better holds. I could smell success, but the rock was streaked with drainage water so I forced myself to place a final runner as disaster insurance.

Dave arrived red in the face, his distaste of chimneys confirmed, but he was obviously delighted with the climb. We spoke in loud voices, reliving each incident of the climb. It was *our* climb, *our* day, and we were determined to wring from it every last drop of mutual credit. You would think we had climbed Cenotaph Corner the way we strutted into the barn that night.

4 Boulders and Training

Try to define rock climbing as a single, all-embracing concept and you risk tying yourself in philosophical knots. Instead, your conception of the sport should grow from what you do in its name, and nowadays that is increasingly likely to include fringe activities such as bouldering, indoor wall climbing and even strength training.

The term *bouldering* collectively describes unroped attempts on miniature climbs. These might be found on small outcrops, at the base of larger crags, or on fallen boulders found beneath either. Some famous problems find their way into guidebooks, their appeal and stature enhanced by notoriety, whereas the majority – charming in their anonymity – await individual rediscovery.

Novices sometimes despise bouldering as 'mere play', whereas the majority of climbers recognise its true worth – not simply as training for bigger things, useful though it is for that purpose, but as an end in itself. Unencumbered by ropes and other paraphernalia, some regard bouldering as the purest form of climbing.

I count several boulder problems among my favourite climbs. Whereas I have difficulty recalling the events of some of my Alpine routes, I can relive each micro-second of these cameo experiences. Unconvinced? By nature, this facet of rock climbing evokes obscure and emotive description, but hopefully this plain account of a typical problem will help to establish a proper context for this fascinating game.

Attractively sculptured, the boulder stands three metres from the track. Over the years I have passed this place a dozen times, but in my impatience for bigger climbs I have failed to notice its potential until now. A six-metre wall slices its right side, not quite vertical but apparently holdless. From its top a tantalising finger-tip flake extends downwards for one metre. This will be the objective.

Close examination reveals a surface to the rock that is rippled like sand exposed by an ebbing tide. The rock itself is of medium texture, promising good friction for boot soles on the protruding lower edges of the ripples. So much for the clinical inspection. In real terms the wall will be almost impossible for me to climb – the perfect boulder problem. It begins to rain before I have so much as laid a finger on it; but I can wait.

A few days later I return armed with a bag of chalk and a cotton rag; the chalk is for drying sweaty fingertips, the rag for drying muddy boot soles after each failed attempt.

I have no concept of time passing. Five attempts and an undetermined number of minutes later I have solved the problem of how to stand on the first hold with my right foot. Progress. Unfortunately my arms are spread in a crucifix position, held there by fingertips which grip the sharp edges of cornflake-sized holds. I can see a hold for the left foot, but each time I attempt to place it the slight shift in balance causes the right foot to slither from its precarious position. I try again, this time leaning my body to the right and ignoring the screaming pain in overloaded fingers. This movement appears to delay my downward departure by about three seconds. This might be enough.

The next attempt wins the elusive left foothold. I transfer my full weight to it and straighten. Now I am leaning against the wall while supported purely by one foot placed sideways on its three millimetre edge. I am so excited by this partial success that I fall off. The distance to the ground is one metre. Three times I repeat the opening manoeuvre; three times without success. On the fourth attempt the cruel cornflake rips the pad of hard skin from my left middle fingertip and puts an end to the campaign; but I will return.

For two months the problem lies dormant while I am distracted by bigger climbs and by mundane matters. A spare hour one fine evening rekindles the memory. In the interim, rain has washed from the finger holds all traces of white chalk. With crab-like hands I begin searching the rock for the correct combination. Suddenly it feels right; at once I step up,

make the transfer left, and straighten – all in one fluid movement as if the choreography has programmed itself into my muscles during earlier attempts. With finger strength in reserve I have a few seconds to explore the next move before my foot creeps from its hold.

Despairing of finding a handhold I simply stand up on a poor friction hold to see what happens. It stays! I have a small chance of success. Unable to reach the fingertip flake, I repeat the previous manoeuvre by stepping up on the sloping lower lip of one of the ripples, hands pawing the rock to aid stability. Now I can just touch the lower extremity of the flake. What a disappointment; barely half a fingertip will tuck behind it. For the flake to be of any use I must lean backwards and work my feet higher up the rock. If my fingers choose that moment to uncurl I will topple over and hit the ground on my back. I consider cutting my

Fig 10 Brownstones Quarry, an ideal bouldering venue near Bolton, Lancashire.

losses by jumping off to a possible twisted ankle but instead, intuitively, decide to go on. I sense a shiver of excitement as the commitment is made. The torment of indecision has lasted about three seconds. Now I need to prepare, mentally and physically. In turn I release each hand and dab my fingers into the chalk bag strung behind my back – a ritual act equivalent to the high diver's final breath before springing from the board. Once resettled, the dry grip feels much more secure.

I have made no conscious decision to initiate the sequence but now find myself leaning backwards and swaying to one side. The tension in my fingers increases as I raise the right foot and place it flat against the rock where it is held secure by its grainy texture. The flake edge bites reassuringly into my fingertip pads as I work them a few centimetres higher. At this moment my left foot skids from its hold, the change in equilibrium having deprived it of retaining pressure. Slowly I begin to pivot outwards like a door on oiled hinges. If I do nothing, then in less than two seconds I will pass the mechanical threshold beyond which my fingers will peel from their holds.

With nothing to lose I lean back further, raise the errant foot and jab it against the rock. It stays. Immediately I raise the other foot, kicking it far out to the right in the hope of finally restoring balance. Magically it finds a good hold for itself. My head pounds, but I dare not pause to reflect on the fleeting sensations which flicker and die there like images in a fire. My strength is fading. With a final lurch I pull into an upright position, defying the physics of friction, and claw over the top for some kind of finishing hold; anything will do.

I am astonished to find myself heaving over on a pathetic little edge, wrists quivering at the strain. It places me safe on the flat top of the boulder. For an instant I remain crouched and tense, like a cat about to spring. In my entire existence I have never felt so alive as this.

TRAINING

Bouldering at its best takes place when you desire to climb the problems for their own sakes, but it is none the less true that the training aspect of the game acts as a valid incentive. A one-hour bouldering session is equivalent to a hundred metres of high standard roped climbing, so improvements in finger strength and mental agility can be tremendous. Those benefits notwithstanding, an emphasis on dynamics will encourage the boulderer to neglect the skills and stamina required for leading difficult rock, when the ability to rest between sequences or when placing runners becomes as important as the ability to complete the actual moves. One way to make good this deficiency is to simulate longer climbs by traversing the base of the outcrop – if necessary three or four times in succession without touching the ground. As you begin to tire you will seek out all manner of contorted rest positions in which to relieve the agony of aching muscles.

A familiar bouldering venue is best for training purposes. That way you will spend a greater proportion of your time on rock than otherwise. Boredom from repetition is not the problem it seems because good bouldering involves stimulating, dance-like movements. A useful training circuit will include perhaps a dozen five-metre problems ranging from slabs to overhanging cracks. Interest will be maintained if you can end the session with attempts on an inspiring, if perhaps impossible, 'last great problem'.

The tangible benefits of bouldering can be dramatic. A *VDiff* climber, for example, can sample (and probably succeed on) any amount of *VS* climbing during a couple of bouldering sessions. That knowledge will subsequently prove to be of immense value when exploring routes of a new standard of difficulty. Not surprisingly, it becomes harder to make substantial improvements as you progress further up the graded scale. Instead, climbers who have 'peaked' in terms of technical ability will use boulder training as a means of quickly getting fit and 'thinking rock' after a winter lay-off.

Not everyone is fortunate in living close to a natural outcrop. Alternative venues include stone buildings, bridge embankments and other man-made structures. Some of these sites have had guidebooks written for them! Repetitive climbing and a lack of interesting features would be a major drawback were it not for the ingenuity of frustrated climbers in creating bizarre problems from unpromising raw material.

Wall Training

Another alternative turns the 'buildering' idea inside out to give the purpose-built indoor climbing wall. The recent proliferation of these structures indicates the degree of importance now attributed to regular training by those who aspire to technical excellence. Wall design varies tremendously, not only in the construction of holds but in overall concept. Many consist of a single vertical wall, whereas a more ambitious design will also include overhangs, cracks, slabs and other realistic features. There are now well over a hundred indoor climbing walls scattered throughout Britain, details of which can be obtained from the BMC (*see* Appendix).

Indoor walls generally make poor substitutes for genuine outcrops when introducing newcomers to the sport. Not only do they lack the atmosphere of outdoor rock, but the climbing lacks its variety. Besides, the move sequences are invariably too strenuous and difficult for a complete beginner to cope with. Some walls have the facility for rope protection, but most climbers prefer to concentrate on short problems or low level traverses. In this sense the wall is being used as an all-weather bouldering venue. Exceptions include those bolt-protected structures which resemble actual rock faces and on which routes may be led in the conventional manner. The style of ascent on these new-generation walls – some of which are over 12m high – closely matches that of bolt-protected sport climbing on actual outcrops. The usefulness of a wall depends as much on its administration as its design. Restrictions such as time limits, compulsory use of ropes, and a ban on chalk, all detract from the value of the facility.

Intensive and regular use of indoor walls (i.e. several hours per week, every week) has produced some dramatic individual improvements. There are well-known cases of moderate climbers being catapulted to the forefront of technical achievement after emerging from a winter of wall training. In this application the climber will use the wall to develop finger strength, endurance, and the mental agility to suppress debilitating anxiety in order to solve highly technical problems. However, over-enthusiasm can lead to troublesome and persistent injuries to muscles, tendons and ligaments. Some very good climbers have been forced into premature retirement for this reason.

You can help to avoid injury by preparing with warm-up and stretching exercises for ten minutes or so before using the wall. It is also wise to build up a wall-training regime gradually, allowing tendons to strengthen at the same rate as the muscles. Finally, a warm-down period on easier problems will help ease muscle stiffness.

Exercise

In addition to wall training, you might consider some sort of exercise at home. At present there is some confusion as to what kind of strength training is most beneficial for rock

Fig 11

Fig 12

Fig 13

Fig 14 A heel hook solves this exciting boulder problem. (A meadow of soft grass, just out of picture, awaits the unsuccessful!)

climbing. Generally speaking, effective training develops certain parts of the body in order to improve a specific performance; but rock climbing calls upon diverse mental and physical skills. Obviously the more training resembles climbing movement the more beneficial it will be. Pull-ups, for instance, will be of far more value than press-ups. In fact, the pull-up exercise has been commercially exploited by companies producing bolt-on training aids for use at home (presumably because door lintels lack sufficient strength or sophistication for today's climber).

As a general rule, strength training seeks to develop the muscle fibres by prolonged working of the muscle near – but not at – its maximum capability. Bearing this in mind, pull-ups may tax undeveloped muscles so severely that the exercise cannot be sustained.

Partial foot support will reduce the load (and the likelihood of injury) but increase the period you are able to exercise. Some climbers develop arm strength, stamina and dynamic attitude by speed climbing without foot support up gymnasium ropes or the underside of rung-and-rope ladders. Effective though this is, it places great strain on untrained arms and shoulders with a severe risk of injury.

Some types of training are less directly beneficial but are useful for improving general fitness and flexibility as well as creating a sense of overall well-being. These include yoga, stretching exercises and running. Coupled with these you might also consider adopting a suitable diet to help attain, or maintain, an optimum body weight. Savage weight-reducing diets, however, will diminish your ability to cope with climbing on large or remote cliffs.

Fig 15 The Bendcrete indoor climbing wall at Kelsey Kerridge Sports Hall, Cambridge.

IN SUMMARY

Bouldering

• Bouldering is the unroped climbing of miniature routes on real or artificial rock.

• It is the purest form of climbing, and also a valuable training aid for bigger routes.

• The most engrossing boulder problems are those which are almost impossible to solve, demanding all your skill, strength and commitment.

• A one-hour bouldering session is equivalent to climbing a 100m route at the limit of your capability.

• Repeated low-level traverses simulate the stamina required on a full-length climb, encouraging the management of arm and finger strength.

• Bouldering prepares you for new demands on technique as you progress up the grading scale, and also for the new season after a winter lay-off.

Indoor Climbing Walls

• There are well over a hundred purpose-built climbing walls throughout Britain.

• New-generation walls simulate real outcrops with textured panels and realistic holds.

• A large venue will incorporate both a bouldering wall and a bolt-protected leading wall up to 13m high.

• Few indoor walls are suitable for introducing beginners to climbing.

• Intensive use of indoor walls can produce dramatic improvements in climbing standard.

• Avoid injuries by building up gradually to regular wall training and by sandwiching sessions between warming-up and warming-down exercises.

• Yoga, stretching exercises and running also help general fitness and poise for climbing.

• Ultimately, the best way to train for climbing is to climb.

There is no doubt that training and exercise will help you realise your potential, but unless you have an ambition to rise to the forefront of technical achievement there is no *need* to adopt formal training at all. Besides, the most enjoyable way to train for climbing is to climb.

5 Hard Rock

'There are only two grades of climb,' I was once told, 'those you can get up and those you can't.' A simplistic view perhaps, but one that helps to explain why one person may retreat baffled from a *Diff* while another glides effortlessly up an *Extreme*. The point is that somewhere along the rising scale of difficulty you will begin to encounter problems which make special demands on your abilities. Precisely where these will begin depends on your physique and psyche, as well as on the peculiarities of the grading system, but encounter them you will.

In clinical terms the differences between neighbouring *VDiff* and *VS* routes (or for that matter between *VS* and *Extreme* routes) simply amount to their steepness, continuity, and size or spacing of holds. In real terms those differences make quite separate demands on your strength, stamina, technical ability, motivation, commitment, self-control and equipment. It is the same game but played in a different league.

The historical precedents for seeking out hard rock climbs were established during the earliest days – such was the nature of rock climbing and the character of the people who migrated to it from hill walking. Standards of difficulty in the sport have continued to rise ever since, pioneered by its innovators and consolidated by its mainstream. This upward trend, however, is much less significant than your own progress through the grades.

COMPONENT PARTS

Writers like to explore the mind game of hard climbing but risk alienating readers who may be unfamiliar with the ground rules or terminology. I have resisted the temptation to follow, but will try to isolate and analyse – not too deeply – the component parts of hard climbing. The risk now is in upsetting those who like to preserve the mystique of hard rock. I think it can be justified; despite what you may hear to the contrary, the majority of 'hard' climbers adopt a structured approach to their routes. There is certainly scope for inspired climbing, but even that builds on a clinical preparation.

Inspiration

The inspiration to attempt a hard climb may come from one of several sources. Guidebooks recognise classic status and indicate quality using a star system, but the modern style of writing is so condensed that there is no longer room for elaboration. Conversely, lavishly illustrated route compilations have space fully to indulge their readers with palm-moistening action photographs and persuasive rhetoric. In fact, such books inspire some climbers to pursue the list of routes with the zeal of train-spotters – puerile but fun.

Guidebook writers all too often underestimate the efficiency of word-of-mouth communication within the climbing community. A single enthusiastic climber propped strategically against a crowded bar on a Saturday night can do more for the popularity of a hard new route than any amount of edited eulogising in a *New Routes* supplement to the guide. By these means a modern classic may receive a hundred ascents before the revised guidebook reaches print.

For all that, the most lasting source of inspiration is the rock itself. It could be that an impressive rock feature once caught your eye, or the sight of climbers at work on a test-piece planted the seed of emulation.

Motivation

Inspiration lies dormant until ignited by curiosity. At first it may be the lure of personal status which motivates you to attempt routes of reputation. Inevitably this mellows with time until the combination of personal challenge, climbing quality, and the prospect of exciting situations becomes inducement enough.

Information

Once attracted by a route, the next step is to find out whether or not your advances are likely to be welcomed or rebuffed. You will know from the route grades whether or not the climb is feasible, but that is not the whole story. For instance, you will want to know the nature of the main difficulties and their proximity to protection. It could be that you are prepared to attempt a well protected crack graded E2 5c, but not a poorly protected slab at E1 5b. Sometimes the guidebook description omits even this basic information, so it helps if you can speak to someone who has already done the climb. A throw-away comment like 'protection is good where it matters' or 'not as sustained as Left Wall' (or some other climb you know well) can be worth half a page of written information.

Physical and Mental Preparation

Generally speaking, it is unrealistic to train for a specific route, although you may need to postpone the attempt to allow for some training if bad weather or illness has kept you off the rocks for a few weeks. Don't be fooled by pub bravado, however. More often than not the heavy drinkers and late night revellers are the ones you will see lowering off their routes the next day. It might sound prim to suggest saving the booze for the celebration, but you can't have it both ways. A hard route is challenging enough as it is, without having to cope with throwing up your breakfast on the stance.

I doubt that any two climbers mentally prepare for a hard climb in the same way. I myself try to visualise the crucial moves, purposely imagining them to be steeper and more difficult than they can possibly be. This leaves me hopping with nervous anxiety by the time I reach the foot of the climb, but because the reality is much less intimidating than the dream I soon relax and start to enjoy the relatively modest difficulties of the climb – or so the theory goes!

Choice of Companions

The harder the climb, the greater the significance of the lead – but the partnership aspect is no less important than on easier routes. Obviously you will be looking for moral support from your partners when the going gets tough, but – hard climbs being what they are – you had also better make sure they (and you) know how to stop plummeting bodies.

The partnership works both ways. Your responsibility as leader is to do your best to ensure that your companion also enjoys the day. Sadly, some climbers are happy to co-opt inexperienced seconds as portable belays for their attempts on hard routes, knowing full well they have little hope of following the pitch without liberal assistance from the rope. Ideally you should try to find someone of comparable ability with whom to share the leads and the adventure. If his or her climbing skills and predilections happen to complement your own, so much the better.

Special Equipment

Later chapters cover equipment in detail; here we shall look at some of those items with special reference to climbing hard rock. If you are unfamiliar with these terms it may help to refer back to this section after reading chapters 6–8.

Effective footwear is no less important than strong fingers. High-friction rubber helps, although the actual make of boot is not crucial – despite what the advertisements say. It is more important that uppers fit snugly and that soles flex to suit your preferred style of climbing. In general, the lateral stiffness of edging boots suits precise footwork and small flat holds, whereas the skin-like flexibility of slippers suits friction moves and sloping holds. Between these two extreme examples are the rock boots and rock shoes which emphasise one or other characteristic but which also retain all-round application. Unless you can afford to buy two pairs, your eventual choice will be a compromise. In any event, the aim is to feel confident in what you wear.

You need only experience a hard work-out on a climbing wall to appreciate the advantages of chalk (light magnesium carbonate). Firstly, it dries the sweat from finger tips and palms to improve grip on everything from pinches to jams. Secondly, the ritual act of dipping your fingers before a hard move mentally prepares you for the task ahead – the self-help equivalent of silent prayer. Improvement in grip is less evident outdoors, but worth having none the less. Valid objections to chalk linger on – the search for an environmentally acceptable alternative continues – and it is undoubtedly true that the greatest benefits are felt by those attempting routes in the higher grades (*HVS* and above), but the suggestion that only those climbing above a certain standard *deserve* to use it does not warrant discussion, not least because someone climb-

Fig 16 The Snake (E2), Craig y Forwyn.

ing solo on a hot day may find chalk greatly reassuring on routes graded *Severe* or less. Whether or not you use chalk on a particular route on a particular day remains a personal decision. That said, you may suffer verbal abuse if you use it on certain routes or crags which are traditionally regarded as chalk-free zones. You can help to minimise spillages and overuse by using a chalk bag which has a secure top closure (remember to fasten it at belays, especially if it is windy), by buying chalk in block rather than powder form, and by dabbing the finger tips rather than plastering the whole hand.

Restrictive clothing severely hampers acrobatic climbing movements and yet it often happens that fashion – not function – dictates what we wear. Happily the two coincide at present in stretch leggings, tracksuit trousers, and so on.

The temptation to save weight by using doubled sub-9mm ropes should be resisted.

On complex routes you may find that in order to avoid rope drag you are effectively protected throughout by a solitary 8.5mm rope, which is inadequate if other factors such as rope fatigue and sharp edges are taken into account. A combination of 9mm and 10.5mm ropes may be the ideal; if runner separation is correctly anticipated, the long run-outs on the pitch can then be protected with the thicker rope. Lightness and simplicity become more important in sport climbing. In this case, and because rope drag is now much less of a problem, a single rope of between 10mm and 11mm diameter is the usual choice.

A similar argument can be applied to karabiners. The difference in weight between individual standard and ultra-light karabiners is negligible, but when multiplied by twenty or thirty it is considerable. Concerns about ultra-light karabiners focus on their gate-open strengths, because this is when they are mostly likely to fail (*see* Chapter 7). For this reason it is worth ensuring that even the lightest of your karabiners meets the minimum UIAA gate-open requirement, and at least some must have a higher strength so they can be used selectively when a potential high loading is anticipated.

The law of self-preservation states that the more exacting the climb, the more protection you will want to place. Apart from an overall increase in quantity you will also wish to augment your standard rack with micro-wires (for protecting a hard move when nothing else will fit), and a wider range of sprung camming devices (for the rapid protection of strenuous jamming or roof cracks). At the same time you might try to achieve some consistency in your racking system so you can quickly select the correct protection without having to sift through the whole assortment. Hopefully your enquiries about the route will reveal which size of protection will be most useful and which you can safely leave behind.

Timing and Conditions

Some skill is required in choosing routes which are unaffected by the prevailing weather. Adverse conditions affect all types of route, but if you are climbing at your technical limit you will have nothing in reserve for dealing with poor friction or cold fingers. Even a slight amount of drainage at the rear of a crack can foil an attempt.

A classic route may attract the attention of several parties over a weekend and delays could amount to two hours or more. Moreover, it can be an unnerving experience having to watch someone struggle on your proposed route as you wait your turn below – especially if they fall off! The answer is to start early or choose a quieter midweek day for your attempt.

Sea cliffs are subject to additional variables which limit the choice of route. These include wind strength (big waves), state of the tide, and seasonal restrictions on climbing imposed for the protection of nesting birds. Tide-tables cost just a few pence from stationers and chandlers in coastal areas, whereas provisional dates of seasonal restrictions are usually indicated in the guidebook and confirmed on notices posted near the cliff tops.

Execution

This is it. With considerable effort and determination you have got yourself to the right place at the right time with the right person. All you have to do now is climb the route!

The greatest danger at this point is in ruining your chances by tensing up. The line between being 'psyched up' and being hopelessly 'psyched out' is a very fine one. Think of it this way: you have at your disposal various finite resources – strength, stamina, runners. With your infinite skill and wisdom you will see to it that none are exhausted before the pitch is finished. Does all this sound too cool and calculating? Don't worry, in practice your head will buzz with so many weird sensations that you will be glad of that nagging inner voice which tells you when to rest, place protection and make commitments.

Most hard climbs consist of difficult sequences strung between larger holds where you can rest and place protection. The most common cause of unexpected failure on hard climbs is lack of confidence; in other words an unwillingness to commit to climbing four or five metres without protection. Stopping in mid-sequence to fiddle with runners is self-defeating because it rapidly drains strength. Consequently you become more nervous, want more protection and lose yet more strength trying to place it – a vicious circle. Eventually the ascent loses all momentum and grinds to a halt in a web of runners. Some routes are so poorly protected that they will be climbed confidently or not at all. The potential rewards here – like the potential falls – are immense.

Falls are inevitable when you are pushing close to your technical limit. Nowadays they have become an accepted part of hard climbing, but that does not mean falling is safe. During the climb, that side of your brain which deals with ropework must continually assess the consequences of a fall so that it can arrange protection according to physical and not wishful thinking. Chapter 10 elaborates on this.

A flawed ascent gives far less pleasure than a pure one. The criteria for disappointment are not related to the reaction of others but to your own feelings about the climb. However, most climbers agree that repeatedly lowering off a pitch, resting on a rope, or pulling up on slings

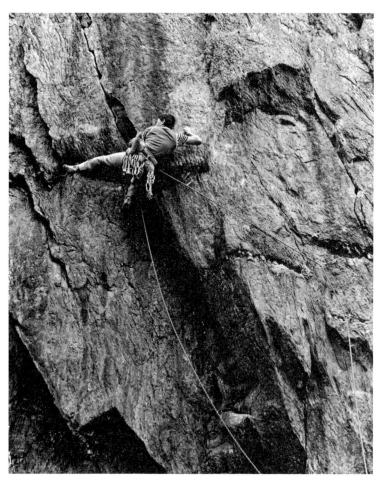

Fig 17 Extreme climbing means staying calm while making precarious moves in strenuous situations. The Pump, an E4, 6b on Clogwyn y Grochan.

IN SUMMARY

Preparation
- 'Hard' rock, though a subjective notion, implies that you will need to make special physical and mental preparations for the ascent.
- Seeking out ever harder routes to attempt is a natural aspect of rock climbing, particularly in the early years.
- A structured approach to preparation for a hard route – splitting the whole problem into constituent parts – is more likely to bring success.
- Supplement guidebook information by seeking advice from someone who has already climbed the route.
- Heavy drinking the night before an attempt firms resolve but wrecks the outcome.
- Mental rehearsal of the route helps to focus your mind.
- Complete trust in your climbing partner frees your mind from nagging safety worries.

Special Equipment
- Familiarity with the limitations of your rock boots is as important as their objective performance qualities.
- Chalk improves grip on handholds and steadies the mind, especially on strenuous routes during hot weather.
- Discriminate use of chalk minimises its unsightly impact on the crag.

- Choose clothing that offers maximum free movement.
- Ruthless weight saving on ropes and karabiners increases the risk of equipment failure.
- Expand your pool of protection gear in both quantity and range, but then save weight by anticipating needs for a specific route and being selective.

Timing and Execution
- Monitor the weather to avoid problems with cold rock, blustery winds or hidden drainage.
- Avoid unnerving queueing by attempting the route midweek or early or late in the day.
- On sea-cliff routes, check for tidal problems and any seasonal restrictions to protect birds.
- Remember that the line between being psyched-up and psyched-out is a narrow one.
- Budget your finite resources of strength, stamina and protection gear.
- Lack of confidence leads to lack of commitment, which in turn leads to overplacement of protection, loss of strength, and ultimate failure.
- Occasional falls are inevitable when pushing close to the limit; don't neglect a clinical appraisal of the risks.
- A flawed ascent detracts from the achievement; back-off and return when you are stronger or more committed.

constitutes a flawed ascent (indicating that either the route is too hard or there is a lack of commitment). The odd thing about this is that you might return the following weekend feeling no stronger but 'thinking positive' and cruise the pitch.

If a lesson is to be learned from all this it is that hard climbs are solved by first splitting the whole problem into its constituent parts. This way you can devote your attention to each in turn with some chance of cumulative success. Otherwise the task may appear so daunting that you are unable to bring yourself to leave the ground.

6   Personal Equipment

There is little point buying expensive equipment *before* you try rock climbing for the first time. The leader will provide ropes and other technical equipment, and may be able to lend you a helmet and harness. Casual clothing and sports footwear should be adequate for the simple, accessible climbs you are likely to attempt on your first day. If your interest in the outdoors began with hillwalking then much of your present equipment – boots, functional clothing, emergency items – can also be used for mountain rock climbs. Nevertheless, once you have begun to climb regularly – albeit as a second – your chances of finding climbing partners will greatly improve if you can demonstrate self-sufficiency in personal safety equipment; that means buying rock boots, harness, helmet and belay brake.

FOOTWEAR

Unfortunately the characteristics of walking boots and climbing boots differ in several respects. As a result you may need to buy a pair of each.

Approach Boots

Most valley crags and outcrops can be approached in sports shoes, but only the treaded soles and water-resistant uppers of walking boots are really at home on the screes, bogs and muddy paths leading to remote mountain crags. Lightweight hillwalking boots make ideal approach footwear and give adequate support on the easiest mountain rock climbs.

Rock Boots *(Fig 19)*

The small footholds typical of harder climbs soon expose the limitations of sports or hillwalking footwear. Only rock boots possess the desired combination of qualities which includes snug fit, friction sole, longitudinal flexibility and lateral stiffness. Each make will emphasise a particular set of attributes, so your choice of boot should also take into account your preferred style of climbing.

Snug Fit A snug fit need not imply discomfort. Your rock boot size will usually be

Fig 18 The EB rock boot, common ancestor of the dozens of species of rock boots, shoes and slippers we see today.

one full continental size smaller than you take in walking boots (but expect variations in sizing between makes). Rock boots sold in half continental sizes offer the best chance of a good fit. Correct length is of paramount importance. When standing, your toes should just touch the front of the boot (but without curling under). This assumes that toe nails have been cut short and that you are wearing socks of medium thickness. Wearing overtight boots on a long climb on a hot day compares with toothache and migraine for unrelieved misery. Later, as you progress up the grading scale, you may be willing to sacrifice comfort for performance; in which case consider buying a second pair – perhaps a rock shoe – which you can wear without socks.

Snug width fit depends as much on the efficiency of the lacing as on the shape of the boot. Check that when pulled tight the lace holes are not drawn too close together, otherwise you will run out of adjustment once socks and uppers have bedded down during use. Unlined suede uppers tend to stretch with use whereas lined or synthetic uppers generally retain their shape.

Sole Friction Sole friction is difficult to assess because its contribution to overall performance, though significant, dominates only on routes in the higher grades. Most rock boots now use butyl ('sticky') rubber soles. These provide more friction than the older carbon rubber type but wear out sooner. Resoles cost approximately one-third of the price of new boots.

Flexibility All smooth-soled rock boots permit longitudinal flexing to ensure maximum friction from the rock in the absence of positive footholds. The degree of lateral flexibility is more variable. At one extreme, the slipper is more like a second skin than a rock boot; foot support has been completely sacrificed for maximum sensitivity. Slippers have only specialised application and are best avoided at

Fig 19 Typical rock shoes. Note the arched sole and narrow, cut-away heel.

first. The rock shoe, a less extreme version of the slipper, retains some of the slipper's sensitivity with its shallow toe, thin sole and cutaway heel, but also provides adequate sideways support. The rock shoe is better adapted for climbing on outcrops than mountain crags. At the other extreme, edging boots provide solid support when applied sideways on small, positive holds. They are most suited to medium-grade mountain rock climbs. The best compromise remains the standard rock boot – direct descendant of the original EB – which shares attributes with both rock shoe and edging boot and can adapt to most types of rock and shapes of hold. The choice in this category is enormous and changes annually.

Mountaineering Boots

Lightweight walking boots lack support on any but the simplest of mountain rock routes.

Conversely, plastic double boots commonly used for Alpine or winter climbing are clumsy for walking and lack sensitivity on sloping holds. On difficult mountain routes it may be best to wear rock boots and carry your approach boots (or trainers if there are no slopes of snow, scree or wet grass to contend with) in a rucksack. Ideal footwear for those who regularly climb medium-grade mountain rock is the *kletterschuhe* – a stiffened medium-weight rock boot fitted with a fully or partially treaded sole. Though widely available in Alpine areas, few shops in Britain stock them.

CLOTHING

Clothes used for mountain rock climbing are little different from those used for hillwalking, except that freedom of movement now assumes a higher priority. Clothes worn on low-lying outcrops need only provide a minimum level of protection and should be as unrestrictive as possible.

Legwear

Jeans or other non-stretch trousers will do for first climbs but are not satisfactory in the long term. Ideally, legwear will fit closely (no voluminous folds to obscure footholds) and yet possess extreme flexibility (for unrestricted leg movements); stretch fabrics used in tracksuit trousers (not the baggy type) and purpose-made climbing leggings meet both requirements.

Midwear

Fleece fabrics provide warmth on cold days but are vulnerable to scuffing unless covered by a windproof layer. Pullover designs are better than zipped jackets. A sweatshirt will be adequate on most days.

Windproof Layer

Unless the midwear layer is itself windproof (which is unlikely) you will occasionally need additional weather protection. A mountain jacket traditionally fulfils this role, but its pockets, zip and hood will impede movement on all but the simplest of climbs. A simple windproof smock in polycotton or similar material makes a better choice. Since this is unlikely to be made from a stretch fabric you will require a reasonably loose fit. A windproof of this type may also be used without the midwear layer in warm weather.

Waterproof Layer

If you insist on climbing in the rain then a simple, hip-length, waterproof jacket in a breathable fabric, and with as few pockets and fittings as possible, would be the ideal choice. Given that snags and rips can be expected, you can save money and improve flexibility – but lose a degree of waterproofness – by wearing a jacket or smock made from uncoated micro-fibre. Overtrousers restrict movement and are probably not worth wearing.

PERSONAL SAFETY EQUIPMENT

Included in this category are certain specialised items which you will need to buy once you have begun to climb regularly.

Harness *(Fig 20)*

In theory, a full body harness or combined chest and sit-harness provides the best support, not only by distributing the load during a fall but also by ensuring that the body does not jack-knife or come to rest in an upside-down position. Both systems tend to restrict movement, however, and most climbers prefer

Fig 20 Main features of a sit-harness: (a) waist padding; (b) waist belt; (c) main buckle; (d) rope tie-in loop; (e) gear carrying loops; (f) leg loops.

Fig 21 Tube-style belay brakes provide smoother rope handling during both belaying and abseiling.

to use the simpler sit-harness. Nevertheless it is important to be aware of the shortcomings of a sit-harness, particularly on routes (often the easier ones) where a leader fall could be unpredictable, prolonged or punishing.

Most sit-harnesses conform to a standard design of padded waistbelt plus leg loops. Some leg loops are detachable so you can choose a belt/loop combination to suit your physique. Others are adjustable for girth, which is particularly useful if the harness is to be worn for winter or Alpine climbing.

When buying a harness it is essential to obtain a correct and comfortable fit. Some are more size tolerant than others; this is something you will need to assess in the equipment shop. Comfort comparisons are best made by hanging from each in turn. A good shop will make provision for this. At the same time you can compare the convenience of gear loops and other fittings.

Make sure the harness you buy is sold with written instructions describing precisely how to fasten the buckles and how to tie on to the main rope.

Belay Brake *(Fig 22)*

This is the device through which the main rope is belayed. It consists of an aluminium alloy disc or tube cut by one or, more usually, two slots. Correctly applied, it will exert a braking force on the rope and help you to arrest your partner's fall.

The brake is used in conjunction with a locking karabiner which you will need to buy at the same time. Most brakes come with a retaining wire or cord. If not, you will also need a length of accessory cord of 4mm or 5mm diameter. This cord links brake and karabiner, retaining the brake in its optimum position for smooth rope handling. This position is approximately 10cm from the locking karabiner for the disc-type brakes.

Fig 22 Belay brake (right) and HMS locking karabiner. The linking cord is usually bought separately.

Nut Key *(Fig 23)*

This inexpensive device assists with removal of jammed protection and helps when threading tape through narrow holes. A typical commercially made key consists of a rigid 20cm metal strip formed into a hook at one end. Some keys also include a facility for aiding withdrawal of camming devices, which are notorious for getting themselves stuck. You might try making your own key from a tent peg or wire coat-hanger.

Prusik Loops

These simple, inexpensive slings formed from 6mm accessory cord are invaluable in an emergency; Chapter 11 has the gruesome details. You will need one of 1m length and one of 1.5m length (allow a few extra centimetres for the knots when buying the cord).

Helmet *(Fig 24)*

A climbing helmet will minimise head injuries sustained as a result of impact with the rock during a fall or from falling stones. Many rock climbers object to wearing them, partly because of the inconvenience and partly because of fashion. Not surprisingly, beginners tend to be influenced by those currently pushing the technical standards of the sport, very few of whom wear helmets. This is unfortunate because, ironically, those climbing on easier angled cliffs are most at risk from loose blocks and the prospect of a long, tumbling fall.

Fig 23 Nut key. The twin hooks are used when extracting Friends.

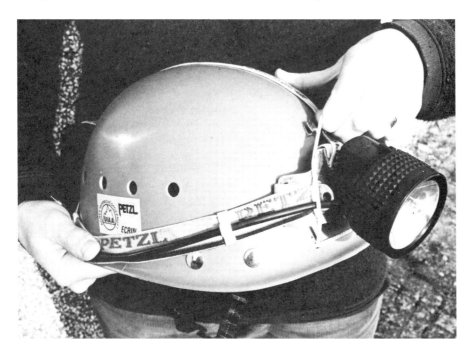

Fig 24 UIAA approved helmet with fittings to secure a headtorch.

A full-weight helmet gives most protection, but a lightweight version is better than no helmet at all. That said, it is wise to choose one which displays the symbol of UIAA approval. This demonstrates that the design meets certain criteria for strength and resilience. Before buying a helmet check that the dome will not easily push backwards to expose the vulnerable upper forehead. If you intend to progress into winter or Alpine climbing then make sure the helmet has headtorch fittings at both front and rear, and that you can adjust the helmet cradle to fit over a balaclava.

MOUNTAINEERING EQUIPMENT

Climbing on high or remote mountain crags calls for a certain amount of emergency back-up equipment, although weight must be kept within reasonable limits – especially if the climbing is likely to be difficult. Your decision on what to carry will take account of such variables as time of year, weather forecast, length and difficulty of route, starting time, remoteness and so on.

Food and Drink

Easily consumed items such as chocolate, nuts and dried fruit make excellent hill food. Water or fruit juice is more refreshing than a fizzy drink, and a screw-top metal bottle a more reliable container for it than the cheap plastic variety, which invariably split.

First-Aid Kit

First aid for rock climbing performs one of three functions depending on the severity of the injury: stabilising the condition of a seriously injured climber until expert help arrives; re-establishing mobility (especially important on a remote cliff); or simply easing discomfort from minor ailments. The first-aid kit should reflect each of these functions.

The best commercially made packs are supplied in water-resistant pouches and include reference notes and diagrams on treatment. Otherwise you might consider compiling your own pack: here is one suggested list (a plastic lunch box makes an ideal container):

Small individual plasters
Roll of zinc-oxide plaster
Crepe bandage
Two triangular bandages
Two large wound dressings
Elastic netting
Paracetamol tablets
Safety pins
Sun cream
Insect repellent
Knife (for cutting slings, rope, etc. for
   improvised splints)
Pencil and paper

Headtorch

Benightment on a big cliff is always a possibility during spring or autumn when daylight hours are few. A headtorch will at least allow you to rig abseils, even if you are unable to finish the climb. At other times it will simply illuminate the return walk from a remote cliff after dusk.

The most reliable torches are those made from a tough plastic and which incorporate a battery housing on the reflector headstrap.

Emergency Bivouac Equipment

It is rarely necessary or practical to carry elaborate bivouac gear. In summer you should be able to survive a night in the open without any special equipment, whereas in spring or autumn a 2.4m × 1.2m (8ft × 4ft) survival bag

IN SUMMARY

Equipment for First Climbs
- There is no need to buy any special equipment for your first rock climbs.
- Later, aim to become self-sufficient as a second with your own rock boots, harness, helmet and belay brake.

Footwear
- Trainers are adequate when walking up to outcrops, though lightweight hillwalking boots are better when approaching remote mountain crags.
- Generally, buy rock boots one continental size smaller than you take in walking boots.
- A very tight fit brings optimum performance but also crippling discomfort.
- Sticky rubber provides good friction but wears out fast. Re-soles cost about one-third of the boot price.
- Choose standard rock boots, combining longitudinal flexibility with lateral stiffness, for your first pair (slippers, rock shoes and edging boots have specialised applications).
- Lightweight hillwalking boots can be worn for the easiest mountain rock climbs.
- *Kletterschuhe* (stiffish, treaded soles fitted to a rock boot upper) are best for long mountain rock climbs of medium grade.

Clothing
- Stretch-nylon tracksuit trousers or climbing leggings provide essential freedom of movement.
- A sweatshirt usually provides enough insulation, though a fleece pullover and windproof smock is a good combination on cool days.
- A micro-fibre smock lacks full waterproofing on wet mountain climbs but is cheaper and more wearable than a breathable waterproof jacket.

Personal Safety Equipment
- Almost all climbers wear sit-harnesses rather than the potentially safer but more restrictive sit/chest combination harnesses.
- Choose a harness with adjustable leg loops if you intend to use it for winter or Alpine climbing.
- Correct harness size is important for safety reasons.
- Make sure the harness comes with instructions on fastening the buckle and tying on.
- A belay brake is standard equipment. It is always used in conjunction with a locking karabiner.
- A nut key aids removal of jammed or inaccessible protection.
- Make emergency prusik loops from 6mm accessory cord, 1m and 1.5m in length.
- Helmets (lightweight, UIAA approved) are rarely worn on vertical, high-grade outcrop climbs but are desirable on all low-grade or mountain rock climbs, and essential wherever there is a stonefall risk.

Mountaineering Equipment
- Compromises must be made in emergency equipment to save weight.
- Nuts, dried fruit and chocolate are more convenient than sandwiches.
- Carry drinks (still rather than fizzy) in metal bottles rather than plastic containers.
- On remote routes, also take a first-aid kit, survival bag, spare clothes, headtorch, compass and 1:25,000 scale map.
- Choose a neat, close-fitting daypack (25–40 litres) with a waistbelt to give maximum stability when climbing.

will protect you and your companion from the worst of the weather. Bags made from heavy-duty polythene are better than lightweight versions in thin polythene or plastic foil (which are unlikely to survive a stormy night, particularly if the ledge is covered in sharp stones).

Spare Clothes

Take what you would expect to carry on a hill walk: gloves, fleece or ski hat, spare pullover, waterproof jacket. Fingerless gloves are useful for climbing on wet or cold rock. During cold weather a thermal balaclava can be worn underneath a helmet.

Map and Compass

The guidebook may give explicit instructions for following the climb but will probably leave you high and dry should you wish to continue to the very summit of the mountain. For route finding among rocky terrain the larger scale 1:25,000 maps are better than those of 1:50,000 scale. A compass will also be required to help with navigation in poor visibility (refer to the bibliography for further reading on navigation).

Rucksack *(Fig 25)*

A rucksack which has a slim, uncluttered, snug-fitting profile is best when rock climbing, although a lid pocket will be useful for

Fig 25 A typical 40 litre daysack in heavy-duty nylon. Note the waistbelt for load stability while climbing.

storing a guidebook and other small items. A rucksack of 25-litre capacity will be adequate for most purposes, though one of 35 or 40 litres would be more useful in winter or for Alpine rock routes. The waist strap tends to foul the sit-harness but greatly improves stability if the climbing is acrobatic.

7 Ropes, Karabiners and Knots

According to popular imagination the purpose of a climbing rope is to drag all members of the party to their death – unless, of course, it snaps at an opportune moment and spares the hero. If you prefer to exert some control over your destiny then observe this four point plan:

1. Understand the physical properties of climbing rope.
2. Choose the correct rope for your needs.
3. Take care of your rope.
4. Apply your rope correctly.

Points one to three we can cover immediately; point four will be discussed at length in Chapter 10.

ROPE SCIENCE *(Fig 26)*

The first climbing ropes were made from twisted hemp fibres. These lacked the capacity to absorb energy and would break under the force of a severe fall, unless the belayer had the presence of mind to arrest the fall gradually. The introduction of nylon after the Second World War brought valuable additional elasticity to the hawser-laid construction.

Hawser-laid nylon has since been superseded by ropes of *kernmantel* structure first developed on the Continent during the 1950s. In this construction a softly laid core (*kern*) is surrounded by a protective braided sheath (*mantel*) to produce a flexible rope with excellent handling characteristics.

Continuous nylon fibres are inherently elastic, but up to two-thirds of a rope's total capacity for stretch derives from the way in which the fibres are bound together. It is this enhanced elasticity which allows climbing ropes to absorb fall energy and hence limit the peak force suffered by climber and belay system.

Although energy absorption is by far the most important property of a climbing rope, it must also behave itself when knotted, coiled, gripped, dragged, climbed up or slid down. Within limits a rope designer is able to control such properties as flexibility, resistance to abrasion, gripping and knotting quality, water

Fig 26 Kernmantel rope construction.

repellency, strength over sharp edges, and elongation under static body weight.

The UIAA has established a standard to govern the most important properties of kernmantel rope. Only those rope types which pass all tests may be awarded the label of approval. The most telling part of the standard is the dynamic test, in which samples of the rope are subjected to a number of severe falls (simulated on a test rig). It is not enough that the samples do not break; they must also demonstrate a capacity to absorb fall energy in a gradual way.

CHOOSING A ROPE

The strength of a rope is closely related to its diameter. The two diameters commonly used in climbing ropes are 9mm and 11mm, although actual diameters may vary by up to 0.5mm from these figures. Ropes of 11mm diameter are used singly, whereas 9mm ropes are used double.

Single rope technique is the easiest to master. Properly applied it is the most convenient method for safeguarding climbs in the lower and middle grades. Despite the possibility of your rapid progression into the higher grades, a single 11mm rope is probably the best initial choice. Later, once the limitations of single rope have become apparent (vulnerability to rope drag, limited abseil capability, etc.), you may decide to switch to double rope technique. However, you only need to buy one 9mm rope as it is standard practice to pair this with a second rope supplied by your climbing partner. If necessary, you could pair the 9mm rope with your original 11mm.

Climbing rope is normally sold in 45m or 50m lengths. Present guidebooks assume the use of 45m ropes and indicate the location of stances accordingly. Ropes of 50m are less popular in Britain, but that extra 5m can prove extremely useful on long pitches or abseils – particularly on the continent where 50m ropes are more widely used.

Having made decisions based on length and diameter, the remaining criteria for choice are less apparent. Rope wears in with use, but you can still get some idea of its handling characteristics when new by forming it into knots, passing it through a belay brake, and performing other standard operations. Suppleness is a much valued property, but not at the expense of a loosely braided sheath which abrades easily and admits damaging grit.

When buying your first rope you are very much at the mercy of the retailer. Providing the rope is of the correct type (single or double) however, and carries the UIAA label, you won't go far wrong. Whatever you do, *never* buy second-hand; every used rope has an unwritten history of misuse.

ROPE CARE *(Figs 27 to 30)*

Nylon climbing rope resists rot but is susceptible to other forms of damage. Careful use and storage will maintain its strength and extend its useful life – and yours too!

Fall Damage

Rope suffers three kinds of traumatic damage during a severe fall: melting, cutting and stress.

The melting temperature of nylon is relatively low and well within that which may be generated when a loaded rope drags across a stationary one. Take extra care when belaying to ensure that the 'live' rope which leads to the climber does not lie over ropes tied to the anchors.

A sharp or abrasive rock edge could cut through a rope during a fall. Guard against this by re-routing the rope away from sharp blocks and narrow cracks.

Fig 27 Coiling the rope. Begin by holding a half-metre tail, then add coils formed at full arm stretch.

Fig 28 Note how the coils are allowed to assume a figure-of-eight shape. This helps to reduce kinking. (Continued in Figs 29 and 30.)

Nylon fibres are irreversibly stretched when arresting a severe fall. Consequently they lose much of their capacity to absorb energy. Rope replacement is the only cure.

Repeated short falls, such as those sustained in sport climbing, stress the rope in a cumulative way. A rope used frequently in this way should be retired sooner than otherwise (*see* Rope Life).

Local Damage and General Deterioration

Falling stones could damage interior fibres while leaving the outer ones unmarked. Rope uncoiled on a ledge is particularly vulnerable. If you suspect damage run the rope slowly between fingertips to check for irregularities.

Embedded grit will cut through interior fibres every time the rope is compressed. Grit can be rinsed out occasionally, but it is still good practice never to stand on the rope.

Outer fibres of the sheath abrade even during normal use. The rope, once smooth and shiny, eventually becomes furry. Although not worrying in itself, this type of superficial damage is indicative of general deterioration.

Care in Transit and Storage

Obviously, climbing ropes must never be used for purposes such as towing or securing luggage to a roof-rack, but there are other, more subtle, precautions to be taken.

Neat coils tend to trap kinks within the rope, so it may be better to allow coils to assume a more natural figure-of-eight shape. Occasionally dragging the rope over grass, or hanging it over a vertical drop, also helps to

Fig 29 Turn back the tail and bind it to the coils with the remaining metre or so of rope.

Fig 30 Finally tuck the end through the tail loop and pull the tail to secure.

remove kinks. It has been shown that feeding rope directly into a bag or rucksack – a method used in caving – is the surest way of avoiding kinks and tangles. However, the climber would then face the inconvenience of having to carry a bag up the route solely for this purpose.

Some chemicals attack nylon. Investigations of broken ropes frequently reveal the cause to be contamination by battery acid. Long term exposure to ultraviolet radiation in sunlight can have a similar effect (which explains drastic strength reductions of otherwise undamaged tape and accessory cord found abandoned on the crags). Ordinary glass is no protection against ultraviolet, so ropes displayed in shop windows or stowed on the rear parcel shelves of cars are also at risk.

Accumulated grit may be removed by rinsing the rope in lukewarm water, after which it is hung to dry in loose hanks away from direct sources of heat. A rope is best stored in a dark, well-ventilated place.

Rope Life

All ropes, however well cared for, gradually deteriorate until eventually they arrive at the end of their useful lives. Unfortunately, there is no reliable means of assessing precisely when that is. As a *rough* guide, a rope used for regular weekend climbing (but otherwise undamaged) will be due for replacement after two years. A rope used infrequently and stored carefully should last up to four years, whereas one subjected to heavy use – perhaps including several minor falls – would be retired after one year or less.

ACCESSORY CORD AND TAPE

Kernmantel ropes of less than 9mm diameter have a variety of applications in protection equipment. The most useful of these cords are those of 8mm, 7mm and 6mm diameters; 5mm and 4mm cords are used for secondary applications such as in harness gear loops. Accessory cord is generally sold off-the-reel by the metre.

An important difference between climbing rope and accessory cord is the latter's *static* (low stretch) property. This accounts for the apparent anomaly of an 8mm cord having a higher static breaking strength than a 9mm climbing rope. It follows that long lengths of accessory cord are poor energy absorbers and should not be used in place of a climbing rope – not even as a top rope on small outcrops. Nylon tape or webbing – being flat and flexible – is especially useful for girdling spikes, threading natural chockstones, and extending runner placements to prevent rope drag. It is sold in widths 10mm to 25mm, in standard or 'super' thickness, and in flat or tubular construction. Standard thickness tubular tape flexes well but knots poorly; thicker tape, though stiffer, resists damage from sharp rock better. Tape can also be bought by the metre, but commercially stitched slings and extenders are stronger and neater (note that the stitching operation is *not* a do-it-yourself task).

Accessory cord and tape are subject to the same kinds of damage and deterioration as the main climbing rope, so preceding advice regarding rope care and replacement apply equally well here.

KARABINERS *(Figs 31 & 32)*

There are two main types of karabiner: *locking* and *ordinary*. Both are made from aluminium alloy bar forged into approximate D-shapes and fitted with sprung gates. The gates of locking karabiners are further secured by a metal sleeve which screws over the latch. On some designs this sleeve is spring-loaded and locks automatically on release.

Fig 31 Locking karabiner.

Locking karabiners are used whenever there is a risk of ordinary gates opening accidentally. Their main applications are in belaying and abseiling.

Ordinary karabiners are cheaper, lighter and quicker to open than locking versions. They are generally used for linking runners to the main climbing rope. The leader may carry twenty or more ordinary karabiners, most of which will be rated at around 2,200kg.

Although breaking strengths quoted for karabiners far exceed theoretically predicted loads, the safety margin is essential to minimise the risk of failure in unfavourable circumstances. It could happen, for instance, that during a fall the load is brought to bear after the gate has been flicked open by a rock projection or sudden tensioning in the rope. The strength of a karabiner is severely reduced when the gate is open (particularly the lightweight types), and if the load is applied through a broad tape – which further exploits its weakness – it may break. (*see* chapter 10 for ways of avoiding improper loading).

Fig 32 Ordinary (non-locking) karabiners: (left) a 2,000kg lightweight and (right) a 2,500kg standard.

Sea water and spray corrode aluminium alloy, so after climbing on sea cliffs it is wise to rinse karabiners in fresh water. There is no evidence to support traditional advice to discard alloy karabiners which have dropped on to a hard surface. It seems this is a hangover from the days of steel karabiners which were vulnerable to internal fracture from this kind of abuse. However, if inspection reveals damage to the gate (such that it fails to close properly by itself) it would be wise to retire the karabiner to a secondary role, such as carrying prusik loops or nut key.

KNOTS

Each of the knots illustrated has several applications. Your decision on which knot to use for a particular application will be based on comparative strength, security and convenience. However, *all* knots weaken the rope to some extent (up to a third) and *all* require checking for tightness. Only essential knots and their main variants (plus a few others of special interest) are given. Some knots may be tied in several different ways, but only the most common are illustrated.

Some knots are secured by a stopper knot. Although this adds nothing to the overall strength of the knot (and in any case frequently comes undone), tying it will at least ensure that you have formed the main knot with a sufficiently long tail.

When buying accessory cord or tape for making up runners you will need to make an allowance for the knot. Assuming that the double-fisherman's will be used for accessory cord and the tape knot for tape, add these approximate lengths to your estimates:

5mm cord – 35cm
6mm cord – 40cm
7mm cord – 45cm
8mm cord – 50cm
15mm tape – 45cm
25mm tape – 55cm

Double Stopper Knot (Fig 33)

Main applications Securing the tail of a main knot.

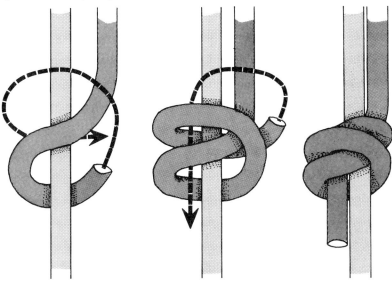

Fig 33 Double stopper knot.

Advantages Less likely to loosen than a simple thumb knot or half hitch (not illustrated).
Disadvantages Consumes more rope than a simple stopper knot.
Special notes Tie the knot very close to the main knot and check frequently for tightness.

Bowline *(Fig 34)*

Main applications Attaching main rope to harness. Tying direct to main rope in absence of harness.
Advantages Easy to adjust for tightness.
Disadvantages Can work loose (especially in stiff rope).
Special notes Settle knot carefully when tying to prevent it from distorting into a slip knot. Secure with a stopper knot.

Figure-of-Eight *(Fig 35)*

Main applications Tying direct to main rope in absence of harness. Attaching to middle of rope. Securing to belay anchors.
Advantages Simple to tie. Versatile.
Disadvantages Difficult to adjust for tightness.

Special notes Secure with stopper knot (unless tied in middle of rope).

Threaded Figure-of-Eight *(Fig 36)*

Main applications Attaching main rope to harness.
Advantages Less likely to loosen than bowline.
Disadvantages Fiddly to tie. Difficult to adjust for tightness.
Special notes Secure with stopper knot.

Clove Hitch *(Fig 37)*

Main applications Securing to subsidiary belay anchors. Means of attachment to protruding pitons to reduce leverage.
Advantages Simple to tie. Easy to adjust for tightness.
Disadvantages Weakens rope more than figure-of-eight when used for securing to belay anchors.

Italian Friction Hitch *(Fig 38)*

Main applications Alternative to the belay

Fig 34 Bowline.

Fig 35 Figure-of-eight.

Fig 36 Threaded figure-of-eight.

Fig 37 Clove hitch.

Fig 38 Italian friction hitch.

brake. Direct belaying. Alternative to descender for abseiling.

Advantages Less vulnerable to misuse than the waist belay. Versatile.

Disadvantages Difficult to offer a tight rope to the second when belaying. Impractical for belaying double rope.

Special notes Best used in conjunction with an HMS self-locking karabiner.

Fig 39 Double Fisherman's.

Double Fisherman's *(Fig 39)*

Main applications Forming loops in accessory cord. Joining main ropes for long abseils.
Advantages Stronger and more secure than the single fisherman's knot (not illustrated).
Disadvantages Difficult to tie. Consumes more rope than single fisherman's.
Special notes When making up runners: allow sufficient rope for long tails (approximately 8 times the cord diameter). Load with body weight to tighten. Secure tails with plastic tape to minimise tangling. Check frequently for tightness and monitor the gradual 'creep' of tails back into the knot (retie if necessary).

Tape Knot *(Fig 40)*

Main applications Forming loops in tape.
Advantages Only knot suitable for joining tape.
Disadvantages Fiddly to tie. Can work loose easily. Less strong and less neat compared to commercially stitched loops.
Special notes Allow sufficient tape for long tails (approximately 5 times the tape width). Load with body weight to tighten. Secure tails with plastic tape to minimise tangling. Check frequently for tightness and monitor the gradual 'creep' of tails back into the knot (retie if necessary).

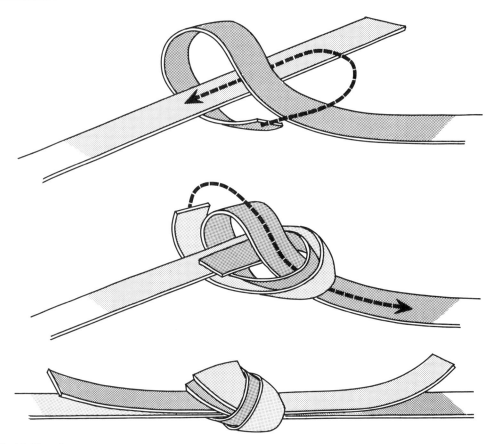

Fig 40 Tape knot.

Prusik Knot *(Fig 41)*

Main applications Temporarily securing the main rope to belay anchors (*see* Chapter 11). Ascending fixed ropes.

Advantages Simple to tie (one-handed with practice). Light, inexpensive alternative to ascending devices.

Disadvantages Can be difficult to release after loading. Could fail if subject to shock loading.

Special notes Efficiency depends on relative diameters: 7mm cord works well on 11mm climbing rope, but 5mm is better for 9mm ropes; 6mm cord is a good compromise.

Klemheist Knot *(Fig 42)*

Main applications Temporarily securing the main rope to belay anchors (*see* Chapter 11). Ascending fixed ropes.

Advantages Gives variable friction (depending on number of turns). Easier to release after loading than the prusik knot.

Disadvantages Difficult to tie one-handed. Could fail if subject to shock loading.

Special notes Efficiency depends on relative diameters: 7mm cord works well on 11mm climbing rope, but 5mm is better for 9mm ropes; 6mm cord is a good compromise. (As a last resort it may be formed using a tape loop.)

Fig 41   Prusik knot (above).

Fig 42   Klemheist knot (below).

57

IN SUMMARY

Choosing Ropes
- An 11mm kernmantel rope is the best choice for first climbs.
- Use double 9mm ropes (or a 9mm/11mm pairing) on more difficult, complex or serious climbs.
- Choose 50m rather than 45m lengths.
- Buy only UIAA-approved ropes and never buy second-hand.

Rope Care
- Ensure that a loaded rope cannot drag over a stationary one.
- Re-route ropes away from sharp or abrasive edges and narrow cracks.
- Discard (or use only for abseiling or top-roping) any rope which has held a single fall of factor 1 or greater (*see* Chapter 10) or held several lesser falls.
- Check the rope after every trip for cuts, internal damage or severe abrasion and discard if necessary.
- Never use the rope for towing cars.
- Coil the rope in a figure-of-eight shape to reduce kinking.
- Discard a rope which has come into contact with battery acid.
- Avoid long-term exposure of the rope to sunlight.
- Remove accumulated grit by rinsing the rope in lukewarm water.
- Dry ropes in loose hanks away from direct heat and store in a dark, well-ventilated place.
- Replace undamaged ropes every one, two or four years depending on use.

Accessory Cord and Tape
- Low-stretch ropes of 4mm to 8mm diameter are used only for protection equipment and secondary applications.
- Use stitched nylon tape for spike runners and for extending wired nuts.
- Discard any runner which has held a fall and replace all accessory cord and tape every few years.

Karabiners
- Use only locking karabiners for belaying, abseiling and crucial runners.
- Use ordinary karabiners for other protection.
- Use karabiners which meet UIAA requirements.
- Rinse karabiners in fresh water after climbing on sea-cliffs.

Knots
- All knots weaken the rope by up to one third.
- Use a double stopper knot to secure the tail of a main knot.
- Use a bowline or figure-of-eight when tying on to the main rope.
- Use a figure-of-eight or clove hitch when securing to belay anchors.
- Use an Italian friction hitch for direct belaying or when belaying or abseiling in the absence of a belay brake or descender.
- Use the double fisherman's when forming loops in cord or when joining two abseil ropes.
- Use the tape knot when forming slings from tape.
- Use the prusik or klemheist as an improvised rope clamp during emergencies.

8 Protection Equipment

This chapter describes protection hardware – slings, nuts, camming devices – and how to place them (pitons are discussed in the aid climbing section of Chapter 12). Chapters 9 to 12 tackle the wider question of how to apply protection to safeguard the climb.

EVOLUTION OF THE NUT

The concept of an intermediate or 'running' belay (hence the term *runner*) is almost as old as the sport itself. A cunning nineteenth-century pioneer would untie from his rope and thread the end behind a stone wedged in a crack before retying to resume the struggle. Thus protected, he might have attempted a gully pitch which otherwise would have been considered unjustifiable. In later years line slings and karabiners substituted for rope threading, while a pocketful of stream pebbles made good the shortage of natural chockstones.

In retrospect the evolution of technical equipment in rock climbing seems exasperatingly slow. It was not until the early 1960s that climbers realised the true potential of artificial chockstones. The earliest type was nothing more than an engineering nut, its threads drilled out to prevent chafing of the line sling on which it was threaded. By the end of the decade these 'nuts' had been superseded by an assortment of drilled alloy wedges and hexagonal bars. The term *nut* remains to remind us of their humble origins.

Fig 43 Hexentrics.

Wedge design during the 1970s concentrated on refining shape and extending the range of sizes. The smallest nuts, being no thicker than the diameter of the finest accessory cord, were threaded onto swaged wire loops – a trend which soon reached its logical conclusion with the brass *micro-nut*.

In the meantime, the regular hexagon shape had been modified into the versatile *hexentric*, in which irregular faces increased the number of placement possibilities to three. Climbers soon discovered that the security of two of these positions was greatly enhanced by the twisting or camming action exerted by the cord. Camming nuts proved particularly useful in the normally unprotectable parallel-sided cracks. The *Tri-cam* further explored the camming concept, while the *Friend* – an ungainly gadget bristling with cogs and springs – later exploited the principle to the full. Here at last was the ultimate nut. Not only would it settle into cracks of variable width but – incredibly – would grip in outwardly flaring cracks. Nevertheless, even the smallest Friend will not fit the finer cracks. The pursuit of 'little friends' continues.

Placement Mechanics

Each sling or nut runner reacts only according to the laws of mechanics. If circumstances demand that the runner fails, then fail it will. Blind faith does not enter into it. What you must try to do when placing protection is to suppress anxiety for a moment and adopt a mental state of clinical detachment. Placing protection is not an art but a science.

The maximum load a runner can withstand is limited by its intrinsic strength. In most cases this is the strength of the cord on which the nut is threaded. Medium and large nuts threaded on 8mm cord are potentially as strong as the rest of the rope system, whereas small nuts – which accept only the finer (weaker) wires and cords – are capable of supporting only gentle falls. The nature of the rock dictates what kind of runner you can place. Some routes are notoriously difficult to protect.

The main cause of runner failure is the nut pulling out of its placement, not the sling snapping. Given that most nuts work on a wedge principle, you can improve security by settling the nut just above a constriction (i.e. where the

crack begins to widen). That in itself, however, is not enough. The force of a fall has direction as well as magnitude. During a fall the direction of pull on the nut or sling depends on the lie of the rope, the site of the previous runner, and the presence of local obstructions (such as a protruding lip of rock). Seemingly perfect runners will fail if the mechanics of the fall exploit limitations of their placement. Chapter 10 details some of the precautions you can take.

Finally, it could happen that the rock itself defeats your best efforts. Runners are placed at points of weakness; when subjected to the force of a fall it could happen that the flake simply peels off, the crack widens, or the pock hole crumbles. This explains why climbers who have grown old and become wise (or more likely began wise and therefore lived to grow old) never put their complete faith in a single runner or belay anchor and instead seek one or more back-ups.

Fig 44 Camming device with flexible stem.

Fig 45 Wired wedges. Note the scooped and curved faces to encourage stable placements.

EQUIPMENT

Long Tape Slings *(Fig 46)*

Type 2.4m tape loops in standard or super thickness, flat or tubular, 15mm to 25mm width, stitched or knotted.

Applications Large trees, blocks, natural chockstones. Often used as a belay anchor.

Limitations Risk of cutting on sharp edges (especially those of standard thickness) and jamming during removal. Bulky to carry.

Recommendation Two ready-stitched 2.4m × 25mm super-thickness tape slings.

Placement Check for sharp edges on blocks and reposition or pad the edge using the knot tails or doubled stitched section.

Fig 46 Long tape slings.

Precautions Broad tape loads karabiners unfavourably so use with a heavy-duty locking karabiner.

Standard Tape Slings *(Fig 47)*

Type 1.2m tape loops in standard or super thickness, flat or tubular, 15mm to 25mm width, stitched or knotted.

Applications Flakes, small spikes, natural chockstones and threads. Also for extending other runners.

Limitations Standard tape is especially

Fig 47 Standard tape slings.

vulnerable to cutting on sharp edges. Super-tape is better in this respect but may be too thick to place around some flakes and threads.
Recommendation Two or three ready-stitched 1.2m × 18mm super-thickness tape slings plus one 0.5m knotted 15mm standard-thickness tape sling for constricted placements.
Placement Beware of creaking flakes and rattling spikes. Check for sharp edges and reposition or pad the edge using the knot tails or doubled stitched section.
Precautions Use a longer sling if the angle made by the tape at the karabiner exceeds about 60 degrees.

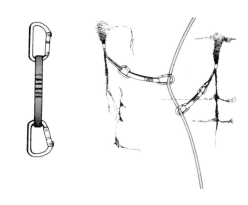

Fig 48 Tape extenders.

Tape Extenders *(Fig 48)*

Type 10cm to 25cm (doubled length) tape loops in standard or super thickness, flat or tubular, 12mm to 25mm width, stitched or knotted, open loop or stitched, standard or shock absorbing.
Applications Extending wired nuts to prevent dislodging and to reduce rope drag. Shock absorbing extenders are claimed to protect suspect placements from shock loading.
Limitations Short loops cannot be used for other applications (small flakes and threads). Broad tape places undue strain on lightweight karabiners.
Recommendation Three or four 12cm × 18mm ready-stitched extenders, plus two 20cm × 15mm ready-stitched open-loop tape slings.
Placement Used in conjunction with karabiners as a link from wire runner to main rope.
Precautions Never loop directly around wire (great risk of cutting).

Wedges *(Fig 49)*

Type Curved or straight faced aluminium alloy wedges drilled to accept 5mm to 8mm diameter accessory cord.
Applications Widely used for runners and

Fig 49 Wedges.

belay anchors in vertical or horizontal cracks, pock holes, pockets, slots, etc.
Limitations Require positive taper for the wedging action to apply. Straight faced wedges are difficult to settle in irregular or crystal choked cracks. Small sizes on 5mm or 6mm cord will not sustain large loads.
Recommendation Graduated range of two or three curved-face wedges on 7mm and 8mm accessory cord.
Placement Look for constrictions in the crack which will prevent outward as well as downward movement. Settle the scooped face around protrusions to minimise swivelling.

The wide placement options (i.e. using the two side faces) are generally less stable.

Precautions Cracks behind blocks and spikes may expand under load and release the wedge. Mud or crystals in the crack may give false placements. Beware of sharp edges to the crack over which the sling may lie (especially in horizontal placements).

Wired Wedges *(Fig 50)*

Type Curved or straight faced aluminium alloy wedges threaded on 2mm to 4mm diameter wire loops.

Applications As for wedges on cord, but also used to protect narrower cracks.

Limitations Vulnerable to being swivelled out by normal rope pull. Small sizes are unable to withstand large loads.

Recommendation Graduated range of about six small and medium sized curved face wedges to complement the selection of wedges on cord.

Placement As for wedges on cord (plus more possibilities for placing higher or deeper in cracks). Settle with a sharp tug; but be prepared in case it suddenly pulls out!

Precautions Minimise swivelling and rope drag by extending each placement. Carry a nut key to aid removal.

Micro-nuts *(Fig 51)*

Type Straight or scoop faced brass wedges soldered on to 1.5mm to 3mm wire loops.

Applications Additional nearby protection for hard moves.

Limitations Low load capability, especially in small size. Require clean and positively tapered cracks. Difficult to remove if placed deep in cracks.

Recommendation Graduated range of three or four (perhaps omitting the smallest and largest sizes) to complement the selection of wired wedges.

Fig 50 Wired wedges.

Placement As for wired wedges, but it is particularly important to choose and settle the placement carefully.

Precautions Minimise swivelling and rope drag by extending each placement. Check the wire for fraying at its junction with the wedge.

Hexs *(Fig 52)*

Type Irregular hexagon alloy bar drilled to accept 5mm to 8mm diameter accessory cord.

Applications Widely used in all types of cracks and pockets (up to fist width) for protection and belay anchors. Particularly useful in horizontal slots. May also be used to protect parallel-sided cracks.

Fig 51 Micro-nuts.

Fig 52 Hexentrics.

Fig 53 Camming devices.

Limitations Require more considered placement than wedges. Ineffective on very shallow cracks. Small sizes are unable to withstand large loads.

Recommendation Selection of three or four medium to medium-large sized Hexentrics on 7mm and 8mm cord.

Placement Look first for constrictions or slots which will give a wedge-like placement. In parallel-sided cracks, settle the faces carefully (using one of two width options) and tug the cord to initiate the camming action. The wide (transverse) placement option acts simply as a wedge.

Precautions As for wedges on cord.

Camming Devices *(Fig 53)*

Type Expanding nuts consisting of a spindle fitted with single, double, triple, or quadruple metal cams.

Applications For fast placement when protecting strenuous pitches – jamming cracks, roofs, etc. Also for placement in parallel or outwardly flaring cracks, pockets and slots, and as a weight saving alternative to several large Hexentrics.

Limitations Expensive and heavy unless replacing several Hexentrics. Ineffective in shallow cracks. May be difficult to remove.

Recommendation Graduated range of up to four medium-sized Friends or other quadruple-cam devices.

Placement Try to optimise the placement by settling the cams in a positively tapering part of the crack and using flared placements only as a last resort. Align the stem or wire frame with the probable direction of rope pull during a fall. Avoid placements near the minimum and maximum of the expansion range.

Precautions Take care to minimise leverage on rigid stems in horizontal placements by placing deeper or by tying off with a sling (as for protruding pitons – refer to the aid climbing section of Chapter 12). Carry a nut key which incorporates a facility for aiding removal of Friends.

BUILDING UP A RACK

Buying a full rack of protection gear at the outset will prove costly. Moreover, you will need only a basic selection at first. The following list suggests a means of progressing gradually from a basic to a comprehensive rack. Note that cord slings fitted to nuts will be about 50 to 60cm long (doubled length). When buying cord remember to make the appropriate allowance for tying the knot.

Basic

For first climbs on outcrops, simple multi-pitch mountain rock climbs, etc.
2 × 2.4m/25mm ready-stitched super-thick-ness tapes
2 × 2,500kg+ locking karabiners (for above)
2 × 1.2m/18mm ready-stitched super-thick-ness tapes
2 × 2,500kg+ ordinary karabiners (for above)
1 × medium-large hex on 8mm cord
1 × size 8 wedge on 8mm cord
1 × size 7 wedge on 8mm cord
1 × size 6 wedge on wire
1 × size 5 wedge on wire
1 × size 4 wedge on wire
5 × 2,200kg+ ordinary karabiners (for above)

Intermediate

Multi-pitch climbs of medium difficulty. As above plus:
1 × medium camming device
1 × medium-large camming device
1 × medium hex on 7mm cord
1 × medium-small hex on 6mm cord
1 × size 3 wedge on wire
1 × size 2 wedge on wire
1 × size 1 wedge on wire
1 × 50cm/15mm knotted standard tape
3 × 12cm/18mm stitched extenders
9 × 2,200kg+ ordinary karabiners (for above)

Comprehensive

All types of high-standard climbs. As above plus:
1 × medium-small camming device
1 × size 4 micro-nut
1 × size 3 micro-nut
1 × size 2 micro-nut
1 × size 1 micro-nut
2 × 10cm/15mm stitched extenders
6 × 2,200kg+ ordinary karabiners

Racking Gear

Protection gear may be racked on a single or twin bandoleer slung over the shoulders (accessible, but gets in the way on low angle rock), or on gear loops fitted to the harness waistbelt (stable, but sometimes awkward to select). Tape slings are generally carried around the neck (easy to remove with either hand but a small risk of strangulation during a fall), or over one shoulder (neater, but cannot be removed by that hand). Long slings are carried double by first twisting into a figure-of-eight shape and clipping the karabiner through both loops thus formed. This prevents loss of the karabiner when the sling is opened out into a single loop.

It is a good idea to rack your runners consistently in some sort of logical order. You will then know precisely what sizes you have and where to find them, even when under pressure on a difficult or strenuous pitch. A typical arrangement would be as follows:

Left side (from front to rear) Hexentrics and camming devices (smallest to front).
Right side (from front to rear) Micros on single karabiner; short extenders pre-clipped with two karabiners; wired wedges on single karabiner; long extenders on single karabiner; chain of spare karabiners; wedges (smallest to front).
Rear Belay brake on locking karabiner; prusik loops and nut key on karabiner.

To avoid confusion when pooling equipment with companions it is a good idea to personalise all your runners and karabiners with a band of coloured insulating tape.

IN SUMMARY

Protection Placement

- Fixing protection is a science not an art and is subject to the laws of mechanics.
- Micro-nuts and nuts on 4mm to 6mm cord can withstand only minor falls.
- Poor placement is the main cause of protection failure.
- Settle wedges above crack constrictions whenever possible.
- Check that protection will withstand a sideways or outward force during a fall and not merely a downward pull.
- Fix back-ups before making a long run-out beyond protection.

Tape Slings

- Avoid placing tape over sharp edges (use the double-thickness stitched section here if unavoidable).
- Use heavy-duty karabiners with broad tapes.
- Use a longer sling if the angle at the karabiner exceeds 60 degrees.
- Never thread tape direct through a wire loop when extending protection; use an extra karabiner instead.

Wedges

- Curved or scoop-faced wedges settle more securely than straight-faced wedges in irregular cracks.
- Use the more stable narrow-profile placement option whenever possible.
- Beware of expanding cracks behind flakes and blocks.
- Extend all wired wedge placements to prevent swivel.
- Settle wired wedges with a tug.
- Carry a nut key to aid wedge removal.

Hexs and Camming Devices

- Hexs are a cheaper, lighter but less versatile alternative to camming devices.
- Camming devices with rigid stems and four cams are generally more stable then those with flexible frames and fewer cams.
- Use camming devices to save energy when protecting strenuous jamming cracks or roof sequences.
- Use parallel or flared placements only as a last resort.
- Avoid placements at the minimum or maximum ends of the camming range.
- Minimise leverage on stems by extending or tying off.

Building up a Rack

- Minimise initial expense and later duplication by building up a rack progressively.
- For simple climbs, concentrate on tape slings and medium-sized wedges.
- For intermediate climbs, add smaller wired wedges, a couple of camming devices, and boost the number of karabiners.
- For harder climbs, fill out the range of camming devices, add micro-nuts, and complete the selection of extenders.

Racking Protection Gear

- Nuts racked on bandoleers remain accessible but obscure vision on low-angled rock; here harness loops are better.
- Carry slings around the neck for easy access and to avoid tangles.
- Rack protection in a consistent order to avoid confusion during urgent placements.
- Personalise your protection gear with marker tape.

9 Rock and Rock Climbing Technique

In grappling too soon with the technicalities of ropework you risk obscuring the essential nature of rock climbing. Besides, it was probably the thought of clinging to steep walls which attracted you to the sport in the first place, not fiddling with knots and metal clips. Perhaps your first taste came during a hill walk when a grassy shoulder suddenly reared up into a rocky ridge, or while exploring the sea-washed coves of a rugged coastline, or earlier still as a child climbing trees or scaling the wall bars of the gym. Don't let anyone tell you that rock climbing is fundamentally different from any of these experiences – it isn't. What it does do is expand and refine the basic climbing instinct in order to squeeze more sensation from those primitive feelings of daring, fear, balance, effort, achievement and exhilaration. So forget about the technicalities for a while and simply 'think rock'.

ROCK FEATURES

The best place to rediscover and relearn climbing is not on a large cliff but on a fallen boulder or small outcrop. If this is no more than five metres high and has a flat meadow beneath it on which to fall, so much the better.

Unless this boulder is very unusual it will not be smooth and regular like an egg. Instead, one side may overhang while the opposite face lies back as a gentle slab. Perhaps half this slab is covered with narrow ledges, the remainder blank and smooth. The other two walls (assuming this boulder is approximately rectangular) are probably more or less vertical; but whereas one may be pitted with holes like a pumice-stone, the other could be split at intervals by irregular fissures ranging in width from a finger-sized crack to a body-sized slot. Even the junctions between the various faces of the boulder are likely to be dissimilar. The first may be rounded and gently angled; the second sharp like the prow of a ship; the third jutting out in a small roof; the fourth indented by a groove. Each feature is a line of weakness by which you can try to climb the boulder.

Even without knowing anything about climbing you would not attempt to use the same technique to climb the pumice wall as you would, for instance, the wide slot. The texture of the rock and the features which shape it dictate how you must position your feet, curl your fingers and lean your body.

ROCK TYPES

Every move on every climb is unique. The rock climber has a new toy every day. Nevertheless, each rock type has its own characteristic form

Fig 54 This arete, with its good but infrequent holds, demands a dynamic approach.

Fig 55 Note how the body shifts to the other side of the arete to make best use of the good right handhold.

Fig 56 By leaning out on this support the feet stay firm on their sloping holds.

Fig 57 Having reached the higher set of hand-holds, body position reverts to a more natural state with most of the weight taken by the feet.

Fig 58 Corner. The least strenuous method of climbing this smooth corner is by bridging up the opposing walls. Note how the boots are placed flat against the rock for maximum friction.

Fig 59 The left palm pushes against the rock to maintain the bridge while raising the left foot.

Fig 60 The feet could have slipped from their friction holds if the reach for the good handhold had been made sooner than this.

Fig 61 Even though the corner is vertical, it is possible to rest the arms completely before resuming the ascent.

Fig 62 Layback. The start of this crack is too wide for comfortable jamming yet too narrow for wedging. Instead its edge is laybacked to make best use of footholds on the wall to its left.

Fig 63 The body must lean well back to prevent the feet slipping.

Fig 64 The hands are moved alternately up the edge; laybacking is extremely tiring so it must be done quickly and with confidence.

Fig 65 Finally, supported by the positive right foothold, it is possible to pull upright ready to enter the wider part of the crack.

Fig 66 Mantelshelf. Emerging from steep rock onto a flat ledge is not always as easy as it seems, especially when the wall has no positive footholds.

Fig 67 The aim is to attain a body position whereby the weight is supported on straight arms, giving a moment's respite.

Fig 68 When ready, one foot is raised and placed on the ledge – a precarious manoeuvre if the ledge is narrow.

Fig 69 Balance can be restored by reaching up to higher handholds, otherwise the other foot is raised and placed alongside the first.

and texture which will govern the battery of techniques used to climb it.

Rounded holds and bulging cracks are typical of gritstone and sandstone outcrops. Chimneys, grooves and jutting overhangs – many of them disconcertingly holdless – are other common features. Fortunately the friction provided by these rocks is so good that even blank grooves and slabs may be attempted. The crack climbs demand a broad repertoire of jamming techniques coupled with a dynamic approach.

Quarried grit poses a very different set of problems. Vertical walls sparsely furnished with small, flat holds are typical. Most cracks are ragged, narrow and possibly choked with mud. However, the cracks in popular quarries are usually clean and a delight to climb. Good footwork and strong fingers are your best assets in the quarry.

White limestone is generally less reliable than other rock types, especially where there are lots of holds (cracks, chimneys, corners). The rock encountered on open walls is usually less treacherous. Some varieties of coarse, grey limestone are wonderfully rough and solid. Even so, footholds polished from regular use will be slippery. Most good limestone routes take to the open walls on good (if small) finger holds. Although the climbing is usually less dynamic than on gritstone it can be much more intimidating, calling for composure and strong fingers.

Volcanic rock found in mountain regions varies in character from one area to the next. The climbing on some crags is reminiscent of gritstone; on others, of limestone. In general, volcanic rock shares some characteristics with each.

Other rock types – slate, shale, dolomitic limestone, quartzite and so on – are less common. Each has its peculiarities of form and texture, ranging from the geometric smoothness of slate to the abstract texture of quartzite.

OTHER FACTORS

Loose Rock

Rock suspected of being loose must be climbed in a very calculated way, testing each hold for soundness with a sharp rap of the fist. Jamming and pinch holds are less likely to crumble than protruding block or flake holds. Even so, it is wise to distribute your weight as evenly as possible among the holds. It goes without saying that the lunging techniques so effective on solid gritstone are not appropriate here.

Climbing in Mountain Boots

The type of footwear worn also has a bearing on technique. Whereas rock boots and other flexible footwear are generally placed sideways on small holds, stiff mountain boots are applied more precisely, using the front of the toe while keeping the heel low. Although the technique feels precarious at first, it can prove extremely effective on certain types of rock. The skill of climbing in stiff boots is worth developing if you have Alpine ambitions.

Vegetation

Some crags are cloaked in vegetation. These vertical gardens are full of treacherous weeds which look stout but which snap like carrots when used as handholds. Trees are normally more trustworthy, but not saplings which are poorly rooted in cupfuls of soil. Bear in mind that most trees on popular climbs eventually wither and die from the decades of abuse, usually accompanying some poor unfortunate to the bottom of the crag.

Damp Rock

Mud-filled cracks ooze slimy water during wet weather and remain greasy for some time

Fig 70 Chimney. Broad fissures are climbed by a combination of back-and-foot and bridging techniques.

Fig 71 The pressure bridge is maintained by feet and back, or – when raising the back – by feet and palms.

Fig 72 This chimney soon becomes too wide for back-and-foot and so is climbed by bridging. The technique is similar to that used in bridging up a corner, but is generally more secure.

Fig 73 Eventually the chimney widens too far for comfortable bridging and, with some trepidation, it is quitted for more conventional climbing up one of its walls.

Fig 74 Jamming Crack. Hand-sized cracks can offer excellent, if painful, security. Often the most secure hand jam is achieved by inserting the hand with little finger uppermost and, if the crack allows, bending the thumb across the palm.

Fig 75 Inserting the hand immediately above a narrowing in the crack also improves security and saves strength.

Fig 76 When the foot is securely jammed in this way it is possible to rest the arms for a few seconds.

Fig 77 Where the crack is parallel sided, the toe is inserted sideways and then the ankle twisted upright.

Fig 78 An overhang need not be the formidable obstacle it appears, provided it can be overcome quickly.

Fig 79 A bold, confident approach reveals a good handhold above.

Fig 80 Using an undercut hold for the left hand, the long reach is made successfully.

Fig 81 Having made the commitment it is best to complete the sequence before strength starts to fade; a retreat from this position would almost certainly result in a fall.

afterwards. Water also transforms crumbly lichen into slippery pads. Few routes are untroubled by lichen; those climbed mainly on sloping holds are most affected. In an emergency you can improve friction by pulling wool socks over your boot soles.

Corner cracks are the features most affected by lingering damp; ridges, the least affected. Other factors which influence a crag's drying time include: aspect and altitude, proximity of trees, quantity of drainage from the hillside above, time of year, air temperature, humidity and wind strength. On a windy day in summer, for example, the open walls of a south facing crag at sea-level may dry out from a heavy shower in less than an hour. Conversely, the drainage cracks of a high north facing crag may remain damp throughout the winter months.

IN SUMMARY

Acquiring Good Technique
• The best way to acquire a fluent climbing technique is to climb on boulders, small outcrops and naturalistic indoor walls, unencumbered by ropes and the mental demands of safety methods.
• Also practise climbing in stiff mountaineering boots if you have Alpine ambitions.

Rock Features
• Every piece of rock and climbing sequence is unique.
• Climbing technique cannot follow a fixed style but must adapt to cope with a wide variety of rock features.

Rock Types
• Each rock type has its own set of characteristic features and holds, ranging from the rough-grained, rounded, grippy and solid holds of gritstone to the fine-grained, sharp-edged, frequently polished and sometimes loose holds of limestone.
• Test holds suspected of being loose with a sharp jab of the fist.
• On brittle rock, spread the weight evenly and use jamming cracks rather than flake holds.

Vegetation
• Some types of vegetation (such as heather) provide firmer handholds than others (such as shallow-rooted grass).
• Treat saplings and sickly trees with respect and grip low on the trunk to minimise leverage.

Damp Rock
• Water adversely affects friction by bloating lichen colonies into slippery pads.
• In an emergency, pull wool socks over boot soles to improve friction.
• A vegetated, north-facing mountain crag may take a week to dry out after heavy rain, whereas a clean, south-facing outcrop may dry within an hour.
• After rain, routes based on corners, grooves and cracks dry out much more slowly than those based on open walls, ridges and aretes.

Developing Climbing Technique
• Study the captioned picture sequences to learn the basic principles then apply, adapt and experiment with them while bouldering on local outcrops.

10 Rope Technique

Maintaining the rock climbing 'safety net' – the rope and belay system – is a wearying task when you consider that the fall it saves may come only once in a lifetime. However, you can be sure that fate, if it can, will exploit even the tiniest lapse in vigilance.

Most climbers learn rope technique by trial and error, applying it thereafter by force of habit. This leaves far too much to chance. Analysis of the underlying principles of efficient rope technique will reward beginner and expert alike.

For all that, even the best ropework is plagued by uncertainties: misunderstandings, elusive anchors, rope cutting edges. It transpires that the best aids to safety are not elaborate rope methods, but climbing partners who promise not to fall. But when they do – which they will – you had better be ready.

UNDERLYING PRINCIPLES

Communication *(Figs 83 to 90)*

Beginners are reticent when asked to call out 'That's me!', 'Climbing!', and other formal expressions from the climbing vocabulary – especially when their partner is in full view and barely ten metres away. Good rope technique, however, depends on leader and second being aware at all times of the precise status of the other, i.e. whether they are anchored, belaying or climbing. A formal exchange of words (or pre-arranged sequence of rope tugs if verbal communication is impossible) avoids dangerous ambiguities.

Security Overlap

At every stage of the climb both leader and second are in some way attached to the cliff – either by anchors at the belay ledge or by the belayed rope. The principle of overlapped security asks that whenever a changeover takes place – such as when the second arrives at the belay ledge – the means of attachment temporarily overlap. Thus, in this instance the leader will continue to belay the second's rope until the second is safely attached to the anchors.

When actually climbing, this principle is so obviously sensible that it barely warrants mention. Amnesia may creep in at times when the dangers are less explicit – such as when the leader has finished climbing a pitch (but has yet to anchor) or when both climbers have arrived at the top of the climb (but have yet to unrope). Several horrific accidents have occurred as a result.

Belay Anchors *(Fig 82)*

Firm anchors placed at the belay ledge are the prerequisites of effective belaying. That is not the end of it, however. Try to find a ledge which allows you to take up a firm, braced stance; otherwise consider sitting down to improve your stability. Remember that the various elements – the anchors, yourself and the rope – together make up a mechanical system. The success of the belay – in other words its effectiveness during a fall – depends on the success of the system as a whole.

Fig 82 Methods of attaching to belay anchors. (A) Rope clipped through anchor karabiner and tied back to the harness using a modified figure-of-eight knot, which incorporates the harness anchor/belaying loop – see inset.(A') An elongated loop of the figure-of-eight knot may be clipped directly to a second anchor. (B) Figure-of-eight knot clipped into the anchor karabiner. (C) Anchor sling clipped directly to the harness using a locking karabiner. Note that the locking karabiner has been turned gate downwards to prevent the belayed rope from unscrewing the locking sleeve.

There are several different ways of securing to the belay anchors: by clipping a locking karabiner directly between the anchor and harness; by knotting the main rope at the anchor karabiner using a figure-of-eight (or clove hitch); or by clipping a loop of the main rope into the anchor karabiner and tying it back to the harness using a figure-of-eight knot. Whichever method you decide to use, make sure that when you are combining belay anchors you can satisfy the following principles:

1. *Load sharing* – so that the stress placed on any one anchor is kept to a minimum.
2. *Independent linking* – so that if one anchor fails, the holding power of others in the system is not jeopardised.
3. *Tolerance to pull direction* – so that the system will resist forces directed from all conceivable directions (such as an upward or sideways pull after the leader has placed protection).
4. *Escape option* – so that if needed the belayer can secure a fallen climber's rope to the anchors and escape the system (see Chapter 11).

Standard Procedure and Communications for Roped Climbing

Fig 83

Fig 84

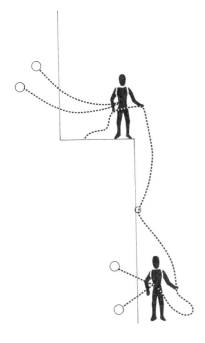

Fig 83 The leader climbs the first pitch, placing runners where possible. The second pays out rope through the belay device, ensuring that it runs smoothly even when the leader moves up suddenly. The lower anchor will prevent the second from being pulled upwards if the leader falls.

Fig 84 Having reached the ledge at the end of the first pitch, the leader begins to place belay anchors. The second continues to belay the rope.

Fig 85 Now secured to the rock, the leader calls down 'Taking in!' On hearing this the second removes the leader's rope from the belay device. The leader now begins to draw up the remaining slack rope. Note that the second remains anchored throughout.

Fig 85

Fig 86 When the rope comes tight, the second shouts 'That's me!' The leader belays the second's rope and then calls 'Climb when you're ready!' On hearing this the second begins removing the belay anchors.

Fig 87 When ready the second calls 'Climbing!' and ascends the pitch, removing the runners, while the leader draws in rope through the belay device. If too much slack rope accumulates the second calls 'Take in!' If a metre or so of slack rope is required (perhaps while removing a runner) the second calls 'Slack!' If a fall is imminent the second calls 'Tight!'

Fig 88 The second secures to the anchors while the leader continues to belay the second's rope. The second will add a third anchor which will sustain an upward pull.

Fig 86

Fig 87

Fig 88

Fig 89

Fig 89 Now secured, the second belays the leader's rope while the leader detaches from the anchors. Note that throughout this changeover period both leader and second are secured either to anchors or to a belayed rope.

Fig 90 The leader now proceeds to climb the next pitch, placing runners as before to minimise the length of a fall. If a rock is accidentally dislodged the leader calls 'Below!' to warn the second and other climbers.

Belay Methods *(Figs 91 to 93)*

As with anchoring, no single method of belaying the rope is best in every set of circumstances. For this reason it is worth learning a variety (*Figs 91* to *93* detail some methods). The waist belay is the most vulnerable to abuse; the Italian friction hitch, the least. All, including the

Fig 90

Fig 91 Belay brake for single rope (brakes with twin slots are required for double ropes). (1) Belay brake; (2) linking cord; (3) locking karabiner; (4) harness anchor/ belaying loop.

Fig 92 Waist belay. In this sequence, from left to right, the rope is being paid out to the leader (in the direction of the arrow). Drawing in rope is similar. Note that the rope is twisted only around the wrist nearest the dead or slack rope. Practise until rope can be paid out and drawn in without uncurling either hand from the rope. Note how the arm is drawn across the chest if a fall occurs (far right). The force of holding a fall will tend to rotate the body; it is important that belay anchors are arranged to resist this effect.

Fig 93 Belaying with a belay brake. Rope is paid out to leader (arrowed) without either hand uncurling from the rope. If a fall occurs, the braking action is initiated by drawing back the braking arm (the left in this example). Note that an obstacle at X, for example a rock bulge, would hinder this braking action; it is essential to arrange the stance so that the braking arm is not hindered in any way. Belaying using the Italian friction hitch is similar, except that braking is initiated simply by tightening the grip in the braking hand.

ubiquitous belay brake, depend on proper control by the belayer. It is a fallacy to assume that mechanical belay devices are foolproof.

The golden rule when belaying is that you must not let go of the rope. Too elementary to mention? Not at all! A careless and unimaginative belayer effectively lets go of the rope every few seconds when paying out or taking in. Regardless of method used, neither hand should uncurl from the rope – at most the grip will relax slightly while the hands are repositioned.

When belaying you may or may not be forewarned of a fall. However, thanks to energy absorbing ropes, the jolt – when it comes – is rarely as severe as you might expect. (The opposite is true of a falling second, when under certain circumstances the jolt may exceed that experienced when holding a leader fall). Provided you have arranged the stance correctly, and at some time have practised holding a simulated fall – be it that of a concrete block on a practice rig or your partner running down a grass slope – then you *will* hold that fall.

PROTECTION PRINCIPLES
(Figs 94 to 97)

The leader places protection primarily to limit the distance of a fall. It is human nature that a leader will climb close to his or her technical limit – in other words risk taking a fall – only when reliable and frequent protection is available to provide insurance in case strength or skill fails. Sometimes the leader will place protection primarily to safeguard the second. This applies particularly to traverse pitches, where the second is equally at risk from pendulum falls.

It would be a mistake to equate directly the potential seriousness of a fall with its length. Certainly the longer falls are more frightening (and more likely to culminate in collisions with ledges) but many prove less traumatic, medically and mechanically, than shorter falls sustained when no runners have been placed. For this reason theorists talk in terms of *fall factors* when describing fall severity. The factor, a number between 0 and 2, is arrived at by dividing the length of the fall by the length of rope available to absorb it (usually the distance between climber and belayer). For example, a leader who climbs above the belay ledge without placing runners and then falls off will experience a fall of factor 2 – which is the theoretical maximum in severity. The jolt suffered by leader and second (and their belay

Fig 95 Runners placed mainly to protect the second. Note that the sling runner has re-routed the rope so that it pulls from directly above while the second climbs the difficult section. The runner placed on the left side of the gap in the ledge protects the leader during the awkward step across; that placed on its right protects the second when making the same move. Note the leader's sitting position to improve stability.

Fig 94 Leader placing runners mainly for personal safety. Note the second's 'upward pull' belay anchor aligned to resist the fall force, which will be directed from the first runner, not from directly above.

Fig 96 Protecting a 'middle-man'. The third climber belays the trailing rope so that the middle climber is protected during the traverse.

Alternative Rope Methods *(Figs 98 to 100)*

Opportunities for protecting intricate climbs, reducing rope drag and safeguarding the second are very much greater when double ropes are used. *Figs 98 & 99* show some possibilities. Note, however, that the two ropes may become separated to such a degree that a leader fall would be held on just one of them. This is tantamount to climbing on a single 9mm rope, which is not recommended. Nevertheless, this need not present a serious problem provided runners are placed at frequent intervals (implying low fall factors).

Rope technique in descent is essentially the reverse of that used for ascent. In this case, however, it is usual for the least able climber to descend first, placing runners for the protection of the second. Clearly this role demands some competence in route finding, placing protection and establishing a belay without supervision.

Top roping may usefully be applied on short climbs when leading is impractical (perhaps because of inexperience among the party, excessive technical difficulty, or unreliable rock). Instead of leading the climb, the belayer gains the top by other means – usually by walking around the side. After fixing belay anchors, the rope end is thrown down for others in the party to tie on and ascend in turn. Alternatively, the belayer may clip the rope into the anchors and then descend (by abseil or other means) to belay the rope from the ground. This has the advantage that the belayer can observe the attempt more closely, perhaps offering advice and encouragement. When top-roping at a popular crag, give precedence to those who wish to climb the route conventionally.

Protection Methods

Runners which have failed – be they slings or

system) will be considerable. Conversely, the leader who slips from just a few feet above a runner when nearing the end of a pitch will experience only a comparatively minor fall. The flight distance may be the same, but the severity – the fall factor – could be a tenth or less. The most important lesson fall factors teach us is the advantage of placing a runner as soon as possible after leaving the belay ledge.

Placing runners interrupts the smooth flow of movement over delicate slabs and squanders stamina on steep cracks. It is often much better to place good runners *before* reaching the difficult section so that on arrival you are able to focus your attention on solving the sequence of moves instead of fretting about lack of protection.

Fig 97 The fall factor increases in severity from 0 to 2. It is calculated by dividing the length of fall by the length of rope available to absorb its energy. Left: the leader has placed no protection and suffers a fall of factor $20 \div 10 = 2$ (maximum severity). Centre: the sling runner placed soon after leaving the stance not only reduces the length of fall but eases the fall severity to factor 1. Right: the additional runner reduces fall severity to 0.5.

nuts – have usually done so because the tensioning rope had flicked them out before the full force was brought to bear. The surest way to safeguard against this is to extend each of the runners at risk with an extra tape sling and karabiner. The more you can do to make the rope run in gradual curves, the better. Apart from 'protecting the protection' this also helps to reduce strength-sapping rope drag. Occasionally you will want to place a runner

solely for that purpose, perhaps re-routing the rope away from a crack or overhang.

Resist the temptation to save karabiners by threading tape directly through wire runners. Wire cuts tape like a knife. Note that the plastic sleeves fitted to some wired nuts do little to alleviate the problem. Nut slings may also be used as extenders provided the second karabiner is clipped into a loop drawn from the head of the nut as shown in *Fig 101*.

85

Fig 98

Fig 99

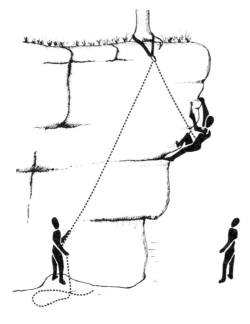

Fig 100

Fig 98 Double rope method. If a single rope had been used the rope drag would have proved intolerable. Note, however, that for much of the time the leader has been effectively climbing on a single thin (9mm) rope.

Fig 99 Double ropes can also improve protection of the second. In this case the second has left one rope clipped to a runner before the traverse to prevent a pendulum fall; the leader pays out this rope while drawing in the other. Hopefully this runner can be flicked off after the pitch has been completed.

Fig 100 Top roping. An alternative to belaying from above is to clip the rope through totally reliable anchors and then belay the rope from below.

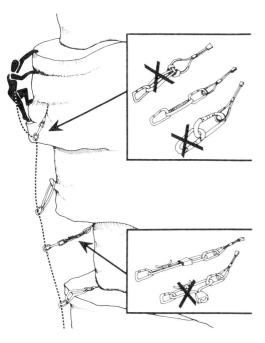

Fig 101 These runners have been extended to ease rope drag and to reduce the likelihood of them being flicked out when tensioned by the normal pull of the rope or by a fall. Note the correct methods of extending wired nuts and of improvising an extender from a nut sling.

Fig 102 Protecting the protection. During a fall the runner placed at the bottom of the crack (inset) would withstand an upward pull, preventing the sling runners above from flicking off as the rope tensions.

Fig 103 Positioning of karabiners. (a) Avoid three-way loadings which stress the gate. (b) Turn karabiners so the gate will not open against the rock. (c) Extend runners so the karabiner back bar is not stressed over an edge. (d) In the absence of locking karabiners, improvise using two ordinary karabiners with gates aligned in opposite directions.

Fig 101

Fig 102

Fig 103

IN SUMMARY

Principles of Rope Safety

• Learn rope safety by comprehending the underlying principles, not by trial and error.
• A single lapse in safe rope technique may prove disastrous.
• Apply a pre-arranged system of unambiguous communication so both leader and second know the safety status of the other at all times.
• Apply a system of security overlap so that both leader and second are always either belayed or anchored.

Secure Belays

• Find a secure anchor and fix one or more back-ups.
• Ensure that the anchor system will also withstand an upward or sideways force.
• Link to the belay anchors using one of four methods according to circumstances.
• Ensure that links to anchors are taut so the loading is shared evenly among them.
• Use independent linking so that the whole system does not fail if one anchor fails.
• For stability adopt a firm, braced stance or sit down.

Belay Methods

• Learn the three main belay methods – waist belay, belay brake, Italian friction hitch – so you can improvise in special circumstances.
• No belay method is foolproof.
• Ensure the braking arm is not obstructed when using the belay brake method.
• Practise the three belay methods until you can both take in and pay out without either hand uncurling from the rope.
• Practise holding falls on a belay weight-drop rig or other simulation.

Protection Principles

• Protection may be placed to limit a leader fall, to minimise a second's pendulum fall on a traverse, to protect other protection, or to minimise rope drag.
• The severity of a fall is measured not by its length but by its fall factor.
• Ensure low fall factors by placing protection as soon as possible after leaving a belay stance.

Alternative Rope Methods

• Use double ropes on intricate climbs to minimise rope drag and to provide extra security for the second.
• During a roped descent, the least experienced climber descends first, placing protection and fixing the belay anchors.
• Top roping on outcrops allows otherwise unduly difficult climbs to be attempted.
• When top roping via a ground belay, the top anchor must be absolutely bomb-proof. Fix back-ups.

Protection Methods

• Extend protection – especially wired nuts – whenever it is at risk from being plucked out by a tensioning rope.
• Use a sling extender rather than an additional karabiner.
• Never thread an extender directly through a wire loop – link with a karabiner.
• Rotate karabiners so their gates will not press open against the rock.
• Avoid three-way loadings on karabiners after threading chockstones or trees.
• Experiment with exotic placements – stacked or opposed nuts – when conventional protection is scarce.

Fig 104 Advanced runner techniques. (a) Stacked wedge and hexentric – tug hard (on one sling only) to secure. (b) Wired nut used to thread a narrow hole. Note that the karabiner clips into a loop of wire drawn from the head of the nut. (c) Nuts in opposition. The overhand knot tied in the right hand sling obtains correct tension between the two nuts. Clip opposed nuts so that if one nut fails, the rope remains captive in the other which may hold.

You might occasionally see linked karabiners used to extend micro-wires, but this too is unsatisfactory. The karabiners may twist against each other, perhaps allowing a gate to open and the rope to jump out. A karabiner gate may also open when pulled against a crack or protruding knob of rock. If the force of a fall applies when the gate is open in this way the karabiner could fail. Guard against this by rotating the karabiner until the gate lies outermost.

A karabiner is also severely weakened when loaded across its width (the 'minor axis'). This is most likely to occur when it has been subjected to a three-way loading, such as when the main rope is clipped directly into the karabiner which joins the two loops of a threaded tape sling. The solution to this particular problem is to lengthen the sling so that both tape loops settle at one end of the karabiner.

A persistent and cunning leader will find ways to protect even the most notoriously underprotected pitch, if necessary by calling on a fund of exotic techniques developed over a period of years. These might include stacked hexentrics, wire threads and opposed nuts. *Fig 104* illustrates a few of the more useful among them.

11 Emergency Rope Techniques

It is in the nature of rock climbing that emergencies will arise from time to time, no matter how careful or experienced you are. Every emergency is unique, so it is far better to grasp underlying principles than memorise a few set procedures.

ABSEILING

The technique of abseiling – sliding down fixed ropes – demands concentration and a thorough approach. There are no grey areas of forgiveness. The list of climbers killed while abseiling (it includes several famous names) makes depressing reading. Abseiling is not a game.

Applications

Abseiling, common in Alpine regions, is rarely used in Britain as a means of normal descent. However, the technique is frequently used when approaching the start of sea cliff climbs. In this case, use a spare rope if you can and leave it fixed in place – you can retrieve it after finishing the climb. In the meantime it will provide a means of escape if your route proves too difficult.

There are other occasions when you might want to abseil the full height of a cliff: when *cleaning* a potential new route (*see* Chapter 12); when researching an attempt on an established but exceptionally difficult route for which prior inspection is considered advisable; or in order to retrieve runners from a pitch on which you failed and had to be lowered off.

Circumstances sometimes dictate that the abseil rope be retrieved from below. A typical example would be an abseil from a pinnacle, or from a quarry climb which finished below a band of unstable rock. Some routes – usually *girdle traverses* – incorporate an abseil in order to bypass a difficult section. In each of these situations you may find abseil anchors (usually pitons) already fixed. That is not to say they will be reliable. Make a fresh judgement and add your own anchor if doubts remain. Remember that prolonged exposure to sunlight severely weakens tape and cord, as does the heat generated during rope retrieval. For these reasons it is essential to fit your own abseil sling on every occasion.

The foregoing are planned abseils. The need to make emergency abseils arises when climbs are abandoned because of failure, falls or bad weather. Your choice of abseil anchor will then be limited by what is immediately available and by the fact that the anchors you place will be abandoned – not that this is a time to be miserly about leaving gear behind.

Methods *(Figs 105 to 108)*

Rope friction regulates the rate of descent. Depending on the method used, this will be generated by clothing, a friction hitch, or by the metal of a mechanical device. A certain

Fig 105 Abseil methods: (a) classic; (b) classic with improvised sit sling; (c) sit harness with descending device, shown here using a belay brake, but the rope arrangement and hand positions are similar when using a figure-of-eight descender or Italian friction hitch.

Fig 106 (left) Figure-of-eight descender.

Fig 107 Italian friction hitch with HMS locking karabiner.

Fig 108 Belay brake with locking karabiner.

amount of friction also develops in the controlling hand; hence the risk of sustaining rope burns unless gloves are worn.

The classic abseil, by far the most insecure and painful method, has inflicted itself on generations of mountaineers. It is nonetheless worth practising because it requires no special equipment other than the rope itself. *Fig 105* shows how to arrange the rope around the body – not recommended when wearing T-shirt and shorts! Take care not to lean *too* far back during the abseil, otherwise the rope under the thigh will migrate towards the knee.

A refinement of the classic abseil bypasses thigh friction (and some discomfort) using a sit sling improvised from a long tape (2.4m) and locking karabiner (*Fig 105*). A proper sit harness takes much of the pain and uncertainty out of abseiling. Refer to the manufacturer's instructions for details of how to secure the belt and where to attach the friction device.

Purpose-made abseil devices offer the best control during the descent. These *descenders* can take a variety of forms, the most popular being the figure-of-eight design. The degree of friction obtained (and therefore the braking force) depends on rope diameter and on whether or not the rope is used single or double. When abseiling on a single 9mm rope, for instance, you will need to create additional friction by passing the slack rope around the shoulder as in a classic abseil. Although mechanical devices are inherently safer than traditional methods of abseiling, take great care not to let clothing or hair be drawn into the device. The disadvantage of the descender is that it is an extra item of equipment to buy and carry.

The Italian friction hitch makes an excellent alternative to the descender and costs nothing. Arrange the ropes through the locking karabiner (ideally of the HMS type) in the same way as for belaying and control the descent as you would when using a descender.

Belay brakes are frequently used for abseiling despite a jerky descent and risk of overheating (a karabiner back bar inserted between brake and locking karabiner will act as a spacer and help smooth the descent). Other improvised abseil devices (linked karabiners, brake bars, etc.) are more complicated and less foolproof than either Italian friction hitch or belay brake and may now be regarded as obsolete.

Abseil Anchors *(Fig 109)*

Abseil ropes placed directly around a block or spike rarely retrieve satisfactorily. Instead, fit a sling over the anchor point and thread the abseil rope directly through this (there is no need to sacrifice a karabiner). If necessary, extend the sling to clear obstructions and give trouble-free retrieval.

Place abseil anchors as you would belay anchors, paying equal attention to the quality

Fig 109 Abseil anchor precautions. (1) Insert piton for maximum mechanical advantage (no possibility of swivelling out). (2) Place abseil anchor sling over rounded edge; if necessary use peg hammer to knock off sharp edges. (3) Make abseil anchor sling of sufficient length to clear obstructions. (4) Join double ropes using double fisherman's knot. (5) Insure the main anchor with a back-up anchor, usually removed by last person prior to descent. (6) Clip the back-up anchor into the abseil ropes so that it does not share the load, but if both anchors are to be abandoned fix the slings so that the load is shared equally between them.

of placements. Remember that the anchors will only be as good as their ability to withstand a force coming from the direction indicated by the lie of the ropes. In this respect it is particularly important to use a spike set high above the ledge to eliminate the possibility of the abseil anchor sling lifting off.

A safety rope protects practice abseils. Arrange this precisely as you would a top rope and simply pay out rope instead of taking in. As a precaution use a separate set of belay anchors from those used to anchor the abseil rope.

In a genuine abseil situation you may not have sufficient rope or time to arrange a safety rope. An alternative is to fix one or more back-up anchors. The last person to abseil will remove these prior to descent, secure in the knowledge that the main anchor has proved

itself reliable. For a true test, carefully adjust the length of back-up anchors so they do not quite support any of the load but would do so without being jolted if the main anchor failed.

The Descent

As a precaution, secure yourself to the anchors while preparing the abseil. Now draw the rope through the abseil anchor sling until the mid-point is reached (but join double ropes with a double fisherman's knot after threading the sling). When using double ropes make a mental note of which rope to pull down during retrieval otherwise the knot will foul the sling.

Tie rope ends together using a bulky knot before feeding them down the crag. If all else fails this knot will stop you from sliding off the end. Avoid tangles by throwing over just a few coils of rope and then feeding out the rest hand over hand. Consider weighting the ends if a strong wind is blowing, otherwise they may whip across the cliff and snag somewhere out of reach.

After fitting the abseil device, but before launching over the edge, check once more that harness buckles and locking karabiners are fastened correctly. There's no coming back! Abseil anchors placed low or towards the rear of the ledge are most likely to fail during the first stage of the descent; if necessary creep over the edge so the rope will not pull at the anchors from a high angle.

The worst moment in abseiling is stepping over the edge. Once established on steep rock and committed to the descent you will feel less apprehensive. Before resuming the descent, check that the ropes do not lie over a sharp edge or in a crack where they may jam during retrieval. When ready, release a little rope through the controlling hand until you are leaning backwards with feet flat against the rock. Avoid the spectacular leaping

Fig 110 Abseil practice using a safety rope. The belayer pays out rope in the normal way; use separate anchors for belayer and abseil rope. Note the body position of the abseiler: leaning back, with feet apart.

descent favoured in public demonstrations (which impresses onlookers but places additional strain on the anchors) and simply walk backwards down the rock, feet apart, while regulating the rate of descent by adjusting the position and grip of the control hand. Note that the upper hand merely aids balance and does not grip the rope.

If you need to pause for more than a few seconds it is useful to know how to lock off a descender (or Italian friction hitch) temporarily. The simplest method is to gather up a loop of slack rope and form it into a simple hitch around the taut rope above the descender. A belay brake is more difficult to lock off because you lose friction while raising the loop of slack rope. Instead, try twisting the slack rope around your leg.

A prusik loop fixed around both abseil ropes and attached to your harness will act as a 'dead man's handle' and arrest your fall if for some reason – such as being struck by a falling stone – you let go of the rope. In these circumstances the klemheist knot is more likely to lock quickly than the standard prusik knot. The upper hand grips the knot during descent, sliding it down to prevent locking. Make sure the loop is not so long that when locked the knot rises beyond reach.

Rope Retrieval

As first climber to descend during a multiple abseil retreat, you will fix the next abseil anchor and secure yourself to it before releasing the abseil ropes. Before the last person descends a trial retrieval of a half-metre or so will indicate whether or not the ropes will pull down freely. If not, ask for the anchor sling to be re-arranged and try again. The last person down must take care not to relinquish the rope ends if there is a chance that they may swing out of reach. After untying the bulky knot, the ropes are recovered by pulling down

on the appropriate rope end. Watch out for falling stones when the rope finally pulls free.

Twisting is the most likely cause of jammed ropes during retrieval. Confirm this by holding the ropes apart and flicking them away from the rock. If after this the rope still refuses to move, the knot may have jammed in a crack. On a one-shot abseil you now have the option of abandoning the rope and returning to free it later. On a long descent, however, you may have no choice but to reascend the ropes on prusik loops and rearrange the abseil. Note that each of these prusik knots must be tied around *both* ropes. It is dangerous to tie off one rope and prusik up the other; under load the slight sawing action of the rope could melt the anchor sling. No easy solution exists to the nightmare problem of a rope which jams part-way through retrieval when one end has passed from reach.

PRUSIKING

The term prusiking applies to any one of several methods of ascending fixed rope. The principle common to all is a one-way knot or device which can slide up the rope but locks when loaded.

Applications

A rare but important application of prusiking is in regaining the route after a fall which leaves you hanging in space or among unclimbable rock. It may be possible to improvise loops from gear you happen to have with you, but it would be better to carry prusik loops already made up into suitable lengths. The second may also resort to prusiking if called upon to complete a difficult pitch in darkness or bad weather. As already indicated, you may be forced to prusik back up an abseil rope if all other attempts to free it have failed.

Methods *(Figs 111 and 112)*

The standard prusik knot (*see* Chapter 7) is versatile and, with practice, is easy to tie one-handed. However, it may fail to work properly in some circumstances – abseil protection, improvised prusiking on tape slings, etc. The klemheist knot is a useful alternative in these situations, particularly since friction can be increased simply by adding extra turns in the knot. There are several other variants, each with special advantages, but these two knots will meet most needs. Except in special circumstances, such as big wall climbing, the superior efficiency of mechanical prusik devices fails to justify the extra weight and expense.

To ascend a fixed rope, first knot both prusik loops to the rope. Attach the short loop to the harness by a locking karabiner, but leave the longer one free, as a foot loop. Note that the short loop is fixed uppermost; this ensures that the rope is in tension (from the foot loop) while raising the knot. The other

Fig 111 Ascenders (mechanical prusik devices).

Fig 112 Ascending a rope using prusik loops. Note that the loop attached to the harness is uppermost.

foot assists the ascent by fending off the rock while you progress slowly upwards.

Sometimes a prusik knot will slip under load, perhaps because of mud on the rope or because the cord diameter is too large. Unless the slide is stopped the loop will melt through – with catastrophic results. Guard against this by tying overhand knots in the slack rope beneath you after every few metres of ascent. The same precaution safeguards against slipping cams on mechanical devices.

A prusik loop must never be subjected to a shock load. A fall of less than one metre may be sufficient to cause failure. For this reason it is futile to protect a solo ascent by sliding a prusik loop up a fixed rope as you climb. Chapter 12 suggests a more reliable method using a mechanical prusik device.

The best place to practise prusiking and discover its limitations is on a fixed rope hung from a tree branch. Only by experimenting with various methods in this safe situation will you resolve the problems that will arise in a real emergency.

FAILURES AND FALLS

A complex retreat after a failure or fall will involve lowers and abseils, demanding ingenuity and a good grasp of the principles of rope security. Some typical situations are described below. A further haunting possibility is the fall which results in serious injury, requiring medical attention and evacuation by a mountain rescue team.

Lowering

Lowering a fallen or failed second down to a resting ledge will cause few problems provided your stance is braced and you are using a belay brake or Italian friction hitch. Lowering a leader involves even less effort because of additional friction developed at the runner karabiner. However, lowering someone from a waist belay can be quite painful when wearing light clothing.

When lowering (or reversing) after a failed lead you may want to retrieve protection as you go, thereby abandoning only the top runner and karabiner. When using a single rope this leaves you without back-up if the top runner fails. It may be wiser simply to lower off and retrieve the runners later from an abseil. On no account try to save a karabiner by lowering on a rope threaded directly through the runner. The sling will melt and break.

When using double ropes you can take advantage of the system by lowering on one rope while being belayed on the other as you remove protection.

If failure occurs high on a pitch (i.e. with insufficient rope available for the lower) the leader may be forced to abseil from the top runner. If the top runner is not totally reliable then a partial lower could be made to reach a better abseil anchor further down.

Escaping the System *(Fig 113)*

In the event of a serious injury after a fall the belayer may need to secure the rope directly to the anchors and escape the system – either to descend to give assistance and first aid or to go for help.

The first priority is to transfer the load from your belay device to the anchors. First fix a prusik loop around the live rope, then clip this, extended if necessary, into a nearby anchor karabiner. If none are within reach, fix a second prusik loop around the anchor ropes and link the two loops with a karabiner. That done, gently lower the fallen climber until the load transfers through the prusik loop to the anchors. Before releasing the belay, reinforce the prusik loop by tying a knot in the slack rope and clipping it directly into the anchors. Now you are free to untie from the rope.

Your next action depends on the nature of the emergency and the amount of spare rope available. If using double ropes, or if the fallen climber hangs less than half a rope length below, you will have sufficient rope to be able to abseil down and give assistance. If not, you may be forced to reverse prusik, probably using the klemheist knot with additional turns to improve grip on the taut rope.

First Aid and Rescue

There is little point in learning elaborate rescue techniques unless you aim to join a local team but you will learn a great deal that is useful by enrolling on a first-aid course. Here you will learn how to examine for fractures and dislocations, to recognise the symptoms of internal injury, and to apply basic treatment. Each

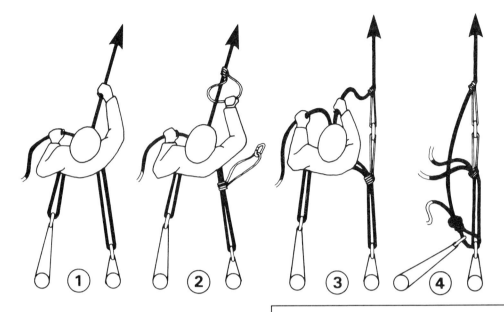

Fig 113 Escaping the belay system. (1) Hold the fall. (2) Attach prusik loops to the live rope and, if necessary, to the anchor ropes. (3) Secure the prusik loop to the anchor and pay out rope until the load transfers to the anchor. (4) Untie from the rope and back up the prusik loop with the main rope and subsidiary anchors.

year a special course is held on first aid for climbers; the British Mountaineering Council will have details. Meanwhile the checklist given here will serve as a reminder.

The International Distress Signal indicates your need of help: *six successive whistle blasts or torch flashes repeated after a one-minute pause.* The acknowledged response from approaching rescuers will be three blasts or flashes repeated after a one-minute pause. If someone can be spared from attending to the casualty time will be saved by sending them down to seek help directly – either from a rescue post (locations marked on some maps) or by dialling 999 and asking for mountain rescue. It is crucial that details of the casualty's injuries and precise location can be supplied at this stage. The requirements are summarised in the checklist.

FIRST-AID CHECKLIST

Check Breathing
If necessary clear airway using a hooked finger to remove obstructions – vomit, blood, teeth etc. Turn casualty to lie in the recovery position (unless you suspect spinal injury). This helps to maintain a clear airway.

Check for Severe Bleeding
Apply direct pressure from a pad to stop bleeding. Elevate the limb.

Check for Broken Bones
Do not move the casualty if a spinal injury is suspected. Immobilise other fractures using improvised splints and slings.

Monitor Condition
Keep casualty warm and comfortable while awaiting rescue (protect from wind and insulate from ground). Reassure casualty and monitor condition regularly.

IN SUMMARY

Abseil Methods
- Abseiling is dangerous; use only if necessary.
- Use a friction device if possible but learn the classic methods for improvising a descent.
- Generate additional friction when abseiling down a single 9mm rope by additionally passing the rope over the shoulder.
- Keep hair, clothing and so on well away from the friction device.

Abseil Anchors
- Abseil ropes placed directly around blocks or spikes often jam – sacrifice a tape sling instead.
- Use a long sling when necessary to ensure smooth retrieval. Avoid sharp edges.
- Ensure that anchors will withstand a pull from the appropriate direction (not necessarily downwards).
- Choose anchors set high above the ledge whenever possible.
- Use a safety rope with separate anchors for practice abseils.
- Use a temporary back-up anchor in the absence of a safety rope.

Abseil Descent
- Secure yourself to the anchors while preparing the abseil.
- If using double ropes, join with a double fisherman's knot and remember which rope to pull during retrieval.
- Tie rope ends together with a bulky knot so you can't slide off the end.
- Feed the rope over the edge to avoid tangles. Weight the end if necessary in windy weather.
- Make a final check of the anchors, harness buckle, karabiners and knots before committing to the abseil.
- Ensure anchors will not lift off as you begin the descent – creep over the edge if necessary.

- Ensure that ropes do not lie over a sharp edge or in a crack.
- Lean back and keep the feet wide apart to maintain balance.
- Descend by walking smoothly backwards – avoid leaps and jolts.
- Regulate rate of descent by gripping with the braking hand, not the upper, steadying hand.
- If necessary, lock-off a friction device mid-descent by a leg twist, hitch or prusik loop.
- Consider using a klemheist knot as a 'dead man's handle'.

Abseil Rope Retrieval
- Fix the next abseil anchor and secure to it before releasing from the abseil ropes.
- Perform a short trial retrieval before the last climber abseils down. Rearrange anchor if necessary.
- Untie the bulky knot and untwist before pulling down the appropriate rope to retrieve. Beware of dislodged stones.
- If the rope jams, free remaining twists and pull from another angle.
- Abandon a jammed rope for later recovery or, if necessary, re-ascend by fixing prusik knots around *both* ropes.

Prusiking
- Use prusik loops to ascend a fixed rope in an emergency.
- Fix the short prusik loop uppermost and attach to the harness; use the longer, lower loop as foot support.
- Tie knots in the main rope behind you as you ascend to guard against slippage.
- Never subject a prusik loop to a shock load such as might occur during a self-protected solo ascent.
- Practise prusiking in a safe place beforehand.

IN SUMMARY (*cont.*)

Lowering Off
- Never lower off direct from a tape or rope sling – it will melt and break. Leave a karabiner.
- When using a single rope, lower off and retrieve the protection later by abseil.
- When using double ropes, lower on one rope and remain protected by the other as runners are removed.

Escaping the System
- Transfer the load direct to the anchors via prusik loops then back them up before releasing the belay brake and untying from the rope.
- If you need to reach a fallen partner, abseil down using spare rope or reverse prusik using klemheist knots.

First Aid and Rescue
- Attend a mountaineering first-aid course to learn improvisation techniques.
- Memorise the check-lists for procedures on first aid, alerting mountain rescue and dealing with rescue helicopters.
- Call attention using the international distress signal.
- Refer to specialised texts and practise improvised rescue if you intend to climb in remote areas.

Rescue teams comprise local volunteers trained in first aid and evacuation techniques. When there is need for urgent medical attention the team may be assisted by an RAF rescue helicopter. In this case someone from the rescue team will advise bystanders of correct procedure as the helicopter approaches. If the helicopter arrives first, follow the standard precautions that are given in the checklist opposite.

When climbing as a party of two on a remote cliff you may be forced into the unenviable position of having to make a choice between staying with your companion and hoping your signals are answered, attempting an improvised rescue, or of leaving to seek help directly. Improvised rescue of a seriously injured climber may do more harm than good. In most cases it would be better to secure your companion from further falls, administer first aid, protect from wind and cold, and then seek expert assistance. Naturally an exception may have to be made if an accident occurred in a very remote area. If you

TO ALERT MOUNTAIN RESCUE

Dial 999, ask for police/mountain rescue, and have the following written details ready:
- Name and description of injured person.
- Precise position of the injured person on the crag.
- Location of the crag, including grid reference and map sheet number.
- Time and nature of accident.
- Extent of injuries.
- Indication of prevailing weather at the scene (cloud base, wind strength, visibility, and so on).

Remain by the phone until met by a police officer or member of the rescue team.

are planning such a trip you should practise improvised techniques, for example hoists and tragsitz lowers. Refer to the bibliography for further reading on this subject.

12 Some Special Topics

This chapter introduces some aspects of the sport which lie outside the mainstream interest. It can do so only in the broadest terms, dipping occasionally into the underlying philosophy or highlighting some special technique. A full treatment would demand a book in itself.

FIRST ASCENTS

Hundreds of low-standard first ascents await those willing to walk long distances and do battle with loose rock and vegetation on the rambling buttresses of mountain crags. This is especially true in the more remote parts of the Scottish Highlands. Even if the route proves to be scrappy it will have been a great adventure as you puzzled over route-finding problems and committed yourself to unknown difficulties. The approach is much the same as that applied to an existing mountain rock climb except that you will need to allow twice as much time, be especially careful with suspect rock and loose debris, and be prepared to abandon the attempt in the face of an excessively difficult or dangerous pitch.

Conversely, opportunities for *on sight* first ascents of major unclimbed lines are rare. At these high levels of technical difficulty, crack debris and lichenous rock will defeat the purist approach so it is usual to abseil down beforehand, cleaning the proposed line with a wire brush and other tools of the trade. Naturally this also gives you the opportunity to remember the location of crucial holds, and maybe even to pull on one or two to see what they feel like. You might also be tempted to test-fit a couple of runners, perhaps leaving one in place to save precious strength on the actual attempt.

All this is very industrious, but pioneering it is not. The irony is that a new route climbed by these tactics involves less uncertainty than an established route climbed by following a guidebook description.

Nevertheless, if your route proves to be a worthwhile addition to the crag people will want to know about it. You can write an elaborate description of it in the new-route log kept at a nearby hut, cafe, pub or gear shop, send a concise version to the appropriate guidebook publisher for inclusion in the next revised edition and, if the route is newsworthy, send brief details to the climbing magazines.

AID CLIMBING *(Fig 114)*

Aid climbing differs fundamentally from free climbing in that you progress up the route by artificial means. It has to be said that standing in slings and pulling up on pitons is not everyone's idea of a good time, but to be fair it will take you into spectacular situations unattainable by conventional means. Except when practised at its extreme, it is a relatively safe, if laborious, way to climb.

Climbers traditionally took up aid climbing during the winter months when the weather was too cold or wet for enjoyable free climbing. During the 1970s, however, most aid climbers defected to indoor walls or to ice climbing.

Fig 114 An aid climb on Kilnsey Crag, Yorkshire.

Aid climbers once dangled and whacked with impunity among gritstone quarries and limestone outcrops. Nowadays these crags provide high-quality free climbs and consequently the opportunities for aid climbing are severely limited. All that remain are a few of the more spectacular roof climbs which so far have repulsed free attempts. Internationally the story is much the same, the more notable exceptions being the vast overhangs of the Dolomites and the blankest walls of Yosemite.

Aid Placements *(Figs 115 & 116)*

Aiding on nuts not only saves time and effort but inflicts far less damage on the rock than banging in pitons. The short, stiff loops of wired nuts ensure maximum height gain per placement – an important consideration on long routes. Placing aid differs little from placing protection, except that now you must steel yourself and trust marginal placements. This is not as alarming as it sounds because of the frequency of protection.

Pitons (also known as *pegs*) are still used for fine, flared or roof cracks where nuts will not hold. Forged from hard steel, they consist of a blade or wedge plus karabiner hole. Blade thickness varies from the wafer-thin *rurps* to fist-sized *bongs*. Pitons are fixed in place using a peg hammer.

Skill and ingenuity in piton placement develop with practice. The ideal placement – and the one sought when using pitons for belay anchors or protection on free climbs – will be made in a deep fault, as opposed to a cracked block or

Fig 115 Pitons: (a) kingpin (thick); (b) kingpin (thin); (c) offset knife-blade; (d) angle; (e) bong; (f) skyhook; (g) rurps; (h) peg hammer.

Piton extraction is a skill in itself. First loosen the placement by hitting the piton eye from side to side (to make the blade swivel). You may now be able to lift out the piton with your fingers. If not, insert the hammer spike or extraction notch and prise out the piton as you would a nail. Problems arise if the blade has bent inside the crack, or if you are unable to hammer the eye from both directions. One solution is to clip a karabiner into the piton and pull outwards on this while carefully tapping the eye.

Popular aid climbs are frequently found *pegged up*, meaning that most if not all placements are already fixed in place. Such routes are fast to climb, provided you have the nerve to trust your weight to rotting slings and rusting metal.

Some of the more spectacular and overhanging routes are climbed almost entirely on

Fig 116 Piton placements: (a) Good placement: mechanically sound and fully inserted. (b) Long piton tied off with clove hitch to reduce leverage. (c) Good placement in vertical crack: constriction below piton. (d) Stacked kingpins as poor substitute for angle piton. In this example, maintain tension in the stack by clipping only the right-hand piton.

flake, in such a way that the plane of the blade is at right angles to the direction of pull. However, when placing pitons for progress (which merely have to sustain body weight) you must be prepared to use all manner of cracks and pockets, perhaps resorting to stacked or tied-off pitons when nothing else will fit.

When selecting a piton, aim to push fit the first two-thirds of its length so that only the final third needs hammering home. A twanging noise when hammering indicates that the crack is shallow and the piton has hit bottom. You might choose another site, select a shorter piton, or tie off the existing one to reduce leverage using a clove hitch tied in a short sling.

Fig 117 Indoor competitions simulate a pure form of climbing in that the route, previously unseen, must be led without rests or falls. There are separate events for men, women, veterans and juniors.

bolts drilled into blank rock. Doubtless these outings will remain popular until such time as the bolt hangers finally disintegrate, but we can expect no more of the genre. Not only would the creation of new bolt routes entail days of effort, but it would attract a storm of protest from ethically minded climbers.

The Aid Climbing Sequence

When transferring to the next aid point your weight is taken in short tape ladders (*etriers*),

whereas when stationary you may sit in relative comfort supported by the harness which in turn is clipped to the aid point via a short length of cord (*cow's tail*). Often two cow's tails are used: one short, one long. On a multi-pitch route, and despite extra tangles, you might secure both etriers to your harness with safety lines. Peg hammers are *always* secured in this way – a precaution your vulnerable second will appreciate.

Ten seconds' delay in one stage of the transfer process amounts to more than fifteen minutes overall in a climb which involves a hundred aid points. Multiply that by the dozen or so stages involved in each cycle and it is easy to see why benightments are common. On a multi-pitch or multi-day route the second will save time by prusiking up a fixed rope (using mechanical prusik devices) to remove gear.

Only those climbers with orderly minds will excel at aid climbing. The first priority is to rack equipment so that it is accessible. A bandoleer slung across the shoulder is most convenient. For optimum speed in selection and placement, try grouping wires on a single karabiner but racking pitons individually. Avoid tangles by relegating tie-offs and extension slings to the harness gear loops.

Orderliness extends to the process of transferring from one placement to the next. This particular ten-point plan is aimed at conserving energy:

1. Stand in the highest rungs of the etriers while fixing the next placement (a short cow's tail maintains balance).
2. Clip chain of two karabiners into new placement.
3. Transfer one etrier to new placement (clip into lower karabiner of the chain).
4. Raise unsupported foot to stand in lowest rung of top etrier (weight still mainly supported by old placement).
5. Clip main rope into upper karabiner of old

placement (this now becomes a runner).

6. Gradually transfer weight to top etrier.

7. Remove short cow's tail from old placement then clip long cow's tail into lower karabiner of new placement and sit back on its support.

8. Retrieve bottom etrier and transfer it to lower karabiner of new placement alongside top etrier.

9. Climb up etriers to stand in highest rungs and clip in short cow's tail to maintain balance.

10. Fix next placement.

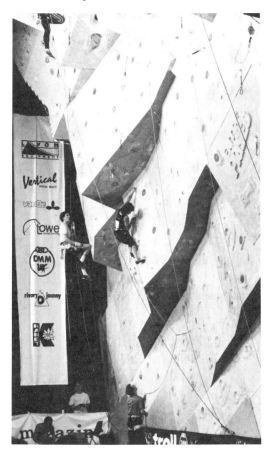

Fig 118 Catherine Destivelle, the famous French mountaineer, competes during the first international grand prix climbing competition to be held in Britain.

At this stage you may not be able to visualise those movements, but it will make sense if you have tried aid climbing and struggled in vain to find a consistent transfer process. Note that the method makes optimum use of the cow's tails, minimises the fall distance if a placement fails, and cuts down on unproductive movements. For all that it is only a guideline. You might use it as a starting point from which to develop your own system. In general, try to satisfy these fundamental principles: maximum efficiency in movement, preservation of strength, minimum strain on placements.

SPORT CLIMBING

Sport climbing allows exceptionally difficult routes to be attempted with very little risk of injury. A typical sport route will ascend a smooth wall of overhanging limestone protected every couple of metres by a bolt. Only those climbers who have developed great strength and stamina through wall training will stand a chance of success, and even then falls sustained during exploratory attempts are commonplace. The object is eventual technical mastery of the pitch. In some cases the route may not even reach the top of the crag, but end at an abseil bolt fixed at the end of the feasible climbing.

Although bolt-protected sport climbs are common on the outcrops of continental Europe, they are confined in Britain to specific quarries and limestone outcrops. At present the general view is that a widespread use of bolts for protection would inflict irreparable damage to the British free-climbing tradition.

COMPETITION CLIMBING

Competition climbing on indoor walls has become a small but established part of the climbing scene now that fears of it spreading to outdoor venues have receded. Major competitions are held on purpose-built leading walls housed in indoor arenas, whereas regional competitions are more likely to be bouldering events held on local climbing walls.

Ironically, both versions simulate climbing in its purest form in that the routes must be climbed on sight and without recourse to resting, aid points or exploratory falls.

SUN ROCK

Few British outcrops allow year-round climbing so winter holidays in Mediterranean countries – particularly southern France and Spain – are becoming increasingly popular. Accommodation is much cheaper at these times, when temperatures are similar to those during the British summer.

It is a myth that most climbs in these areas are both technically difficult and bolt-protected, though certainly this is true for some outcrops, as indeed it is in Britain. Some English text guidebooks do not convey the true mid-grade potential, so it is worth talking to climbers who have had first-hand experience of the country you intend to visit. They may also be able to advise on practical matters such as obtaining cheap flights and accommodation, and equipment needs.

ALPINE ROCK

Not all Alpine climbing revolves around snow peaks and glaciers. The limestone walls of the Dolomites, for instance, or the granite pillars of the Mont Blanc massif present magnificent rock climbing challenges set amid breathtaking scenery.

Provided no snow and ice climbing is involved, you will base your equipment for a one-day Alpine rock climb on what you might take for a long mountaineering route in Britain. Unfortunately these one-day Alpine routes have a nasty habit of dragging on into night.

The classic dilemma is whether or not to take bivouac gear, the implication being that time lost in carrying it invites benightment. At the very least you should aim to carry a survival bag and spare pullovers (or quilted jacket) against the possibility of storm-enforced delay.

A primary consideration will be choice of footwear. Rock boots are fine for short routes at low altitude, but not for long climbs which might include snowfields on the approach or descent. Mountain boots are too clumsy for technical climbing, however, so you may need to take both. A good compromise on medium grade routes would be to wear lightweight but stiff-soled *klettershuhe* throughout. These are rarely sold in Britain but are quite common in the gear shops of Alpine resorts.

Stonefall is an ever-present danger and so helmets are always worn. Make sure you are the first team on the rock, particularly if the route is popular with guided parties who may be less careful about dislodging loose stones from ledges. Take extra care if your climb is capped by a snowfield; it will release rocks as the sun begins to melt its edges.

Major rockfalls are usually caused by the release of frost-shattered blocks due to direct warming by the sun. This can occur without warning at any time from dawn until dusk. Couloir and corner climbs are more exposed to major stonefall than ridge or arete climbs, though none is completely free of risk.

Pitons are used occasionally as belay anchors and often as abseil anchors. As a rule you should carry a selection of three or four pitons, plus two or three in reserve for a forced retreat. Abseil anchor slings can be cut as and when they are required from a 5m length of 7mm cord carried specifically for the purpose. You might substitute a short-handled ice hammer for the peg hammer if snow is expected. Although clumsy to carry on rock, this will save having to carry a separate ice-axe.

Paradoxically, British climbers invite disaster in the Alps with their thorough and unhurried approach to belaying learned on little crags. Speed *is* important in the Alps. Two techniques which help maintain the momentum of the ascent are *direct belaying* and *moving together*.

Direct Belaying *(Fig 119)*

In direct belaying, the Italian friction hitch is tied directly into an HMS locking karabiner at the anchor. Meanwhile the belayer secures to a separate anchor. Although the direct belay can be used to safeguard the leader, its main application is in keeping pace with an athletic second racing up a simple pitch. It goes without saying that the anchor must be 100 per cent reliable.

Moving Together *(Fig 120)*

The technique of moving together is most useful when crossing easy ground between pitches of more difficult climbing – the sort of rock you might solo but for the inconvenience of having to untie the ropes. Each climber takes up coils until separated by 5–10m of rope (the actual length will depend on the nature of terrain). These coils are carried over the shoulder in the normal way, except that the final turn is tied off at the harness using a figure-of-eight knot (to prevent the rest of the coils becoming a noose). After taking up a couple of short hand coils the two climbers move simultaneously, flicking the rope which lies between them over and around spikes as they go. The technique can be particularly effective when moving along an exposed but technically simple ridge crest.

Fig 119 Direct belay using Italian friction hitch. Note separate belay anchor installed to prevent the belayer from being pulled towards the hitch when holding a fall. Belay brakes must not be used for direct belaying in this way, because of the difficulty of initiating the braking action.

CLIMBING SOLO *(Fig 121)*

Common sense tells us never to climb alone, but for those who have the experience to cope with unexpected difficulties, soloing offers unforgettable thrills. Soloing also makes it possible to cover more ground; a confident solo climber can feast on a thousand metres of rock while a roped party nibbles on a hundred.

Few climbers are prepared to solo even within three full grades of their top leading standard, and usually select much easier routes. Even simple climbs offer an engrossing challenge when the consequences of a mistake are so severe.

Fig 120 Climbers moving together along an easy ridge.

Fig 121 Soloing an easy climb in the Ogwen Valley.

Protection Techniques *(Fig 122)*

Not everyone solos for the thrill and freedom of climbing unroped. There may be sound practical reasons why you choose to climb alone, such as when your free time falls mid-week. There are ways of protecting a solo climb on these occasions, although none is entirely satisfactory.

By far the safest method is to hang a fixed rope down the crag and then protect yourself as you climb by sliding a prusik device up the rope. Clearly the method is only suitable for one-pitch routes. Prusik loops are wholly unsuitable for this purpose, and even a mechanical device may fail under the shock load of holding your fall. One solution is to fix the prusik device in such a way that it slides automatically up the rope as you climb. If the route follows a zigzag line you can minimise the risk of a pendulum fall by first abseiling down the fixed rope to place runners at the turning points.

Protecting a multi-pitch route is more complicated and much less secure. First secure one end of the rope to several good anchors (which must be capable of withstanding an upward pull). Now tie a figure-of-eight knot a few metres from this end and clip it to your harness by a locking karabiner. With this dubious protection (if you fall off the force on both you and the anchors will be enormous) you can now set about climbing the pitch, clipping the rope into protection as you go. When the rope threatens to come tight behind you, gather up some slack, tie a knot, and clip this into your harness by a second locking karabiner. Releasing the first knot now frees you to climb another few metres. Repeat the process and eventually you will gain the top of the pitch. Now fix the rope to a new set of anchors and abseil back down the pitch, collecting runners as you go. After removing the lower set of anchors, prusik

Fig 122 Using a top rope and Clog ascender to protect a solo climb. The lower locking karabiner clips directly into the harness anchor/belaying loop, whereas the upper ordinary karabiner clips into a tape sling worn across the chest like a bandoleer. This chest link pulls the ascender up the rope as you climb, whereas the harness link supports your weight if you fall.

back up the rope (mechanical devices for speed) to regain the upper ledge. Provided you still have the energy and inclination, you may now repeat the entire procedure on the next pitch.

A faster but less secure method is to climb unroped, protecting the occasional difficult move by clipping a sling into a runner you have placed nearby (hopefully you will remember to flick this out before climbing too high). However, since no part of the system is able to absorb energy, even a tiny fall could generate sufficient force to cause the anchor to fail. The practical value of this method, therefore, lies in having a nearby sling to grab if things suddenly start to go badly wrong.

Self-belay devices are marketed from time to time which claim to protect the roped solo

IN SUMMARY

First Ascents

- Unclimbed rock can still be found on remote mountain crags, but take special care with suspect rock.
- Worthwhile first ascents on accessible crags will probably be extremely difficult and involve abseil inspection and cleaning.
- First ascents can be reported locally using new-route books and descriptions sent to guidebook publishers and magazines.

Aid Climbing

- Safe, laborious but spectacular progress is made by placing pitons or wired nuts and standing in slings.
- Use wired nuts in preference to pitons whenever possible to save time and minimise rock damage.
- A piton of ideal length and width can be push fitted for two-thirds of its length then hammered home.
- For a piton belay or abseil anchor, seek an in-sloping horizontal placement in an intrinsic fissure (not behind a suspect block or flake), or at least place the piton above a constriction if the crack is vertical.
- Use a clove hitch tie-off to reduce leverage on a bottomed-out piton.
- Extract pitons by tapping the eye from side to side so the blade swivels. If necessary, clip a karabiner to the eye and pull while tapping.
- Aid routes found already 'pegged-up' are fast but precarious to climb.
- An orderly approach both to racking gear and progressing between placements is essential in aid climbing.
- Good aid climbing technique maximises efficiency in movement, preserves strength and minimises strain on placements.

Sport Climbing

- Sport climbing allows difficult routes to be attempted with little risk of injury.
- The process demands great strength and stamina.
- Short falls are commonplace.
- Bolt-protected sport climbs are confined in Britain to specific quarries and limestone outcrops.

Competition Climbing

- Major competitions are held on purpose-built leading walls housed in indoor arenas.
- Regional bouldering events are held on local climbing walls.
- Though the climbing in competitions is simulated, its purity of form encourages a bold, stylish and ethically sound technique.

Sun Rock

- Outcrops in Mediterranean countries offer excellent winter rock climbing with the possibility of cheap flights and accommodation.
- Bolt-protected climbs are common but not universal.
- Despite rumours, there are also good climbs in the middle grades.

Alpine Rock

- Alpine rock in the Dolomites, Mont Blanc region and elsewhere presents serious challenges among breathtaking scenery.
- Unplanned bivouacs are inevitable: don't invite them by overloading, but at least take spare clothing and a bivi bag.
- Ideally use rock boots for hard climbs, mountain boots for easy climbs, and *klettershuhe* for mid-grade climbs.
- Minimise the stonefall risk by wearing a

IN SUMMARY (*cont.*)

helmet, starting at the front of queues, avoiding couloirs, and being aware of sun-warming effects.
• Carry a selection of pitons plus 5m of 7mm cord for fixing abseil anchors.
• Consider carrying an ice hammer instead of a peg hammer if there may be snow on the approach or descent.
• Save vital time by using direct belays or moving together when appropriate.

Climbing Solo
• Solo climbing is thrilling but intrinsically dangerous.
• Select climbs several grades down from your usual leading standard.
• Single-pitch solo climbs may be protected by a top rope and an auto-sliding ascender.
• Multi-pitch solo climbs may be partially protected by self-belay methods.

climber as efficiently as a second using a belay brake. Even so, it would be unwise to attempt to solo a serious route in the belief that you are fully protected. Not only must all the strain be taken by the belay anchors (as opposed to the countering weight of the belayer) but also there will be no back-up support if you fall and sustain an injury.

Soloing can never be considered safe. Each bad mistake rubs out a life.

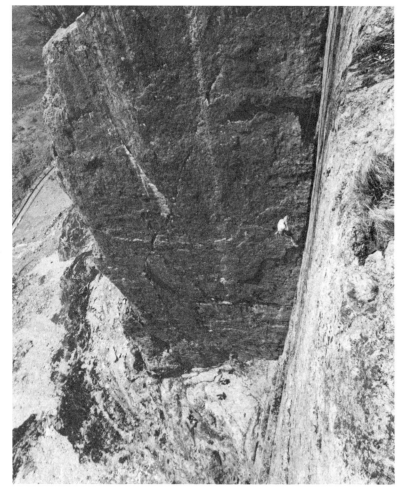

Fig 123 Abseiling down the right wall of Cenotaph Corner.

APPENDIX

GRADING SYSTEMS

Originators of rock climbs allocate grades to their routes on a scale ranging from *Easy* to *Extremely Severe*. These are later confirmed or modified by the guide writer. The grade of a route is the single most important piece of information to those who wish to repeat the ascent. In time climbers get a feel for what grade of route lies within their ability, although naturally this will be modified according to weather conditions, current level of fitness, type of climbing and so on.

The need to differentiate between safe and serious routes has brought about a dual grading system. In this the adjectival component assesses the overall proposition, while the numerical component attempts to assess pure technical difficulty. Aid climbs have a grading system of their own, based on a combined assessment of seriousness and ease of aid placement (since the two are often closely related).

Despite sharing a common system, in Britain it is rarely possible to make direct grade comparisons between the regions. Although first encounters with unfamiliar rock are always disconcerting, major discrepancies remain and so it is wise to approach a new area with caution.

Comparisons between neighbouring routes can be equally misleading. Some climbers excel on strenuous cracks, others on delicate slabs. The guide writer can only attempt to steer a compromising line. The final responsibility – as always – rests with the climber.

Other countries have developed grading systems of their own. Grades in the United States and Australia are entirely numerical, whereas those allocated to climbs in the Western Alps have both overall and technical components. Some European countries grade their outcrop climbs on a separate scale, adding to the confusion. The UIAA have tried to convert everyone to their international system of numerical grades, but with only mixed success. At present it is used primarily for mountain rock climbs in the Eastern Alps and for pitch grading in the Western Alps.

British Grading System

These adjectival grades and their standard abbreviations indicate overall difficulty (note that their literal meanings have been lost).

Easy (E) Mainly scrambling, although a rope may be used to protect exposed sections. Not generally regarded as proper rock climbing.
Moderate (M) Rock climbing in the true sense of the word, but with large holds on rock set at a comfortable angle. A single rope plus small selection of slings and nuts will suffice.
Difficult (D) Entertaining climbing on good holds. Suitable for beginners and for first leads, although the angle may occasionally approach vertical.
Very Difficult (VD) Climbing of a more sustained nature, demanding a thoughtful and enthusiastic approach if beginners are to succeed. There are many good climbs at this standard. Rock boots will be an advantage, and a broad selection of runners will be required.
Severe (S) Steep, sustained climbing on good holds, or perhaps slab climbing with some

poor holds. Complete beginners generally find these routes too demanding.

Very Severe (VS) Sustained climbing encompassing all kinds of features and techniques, probably with several baffling moves. An enthusiastic beginner could be climbing these routes within a year. There are many famous routes at this grade. A comprehensive set of runners will be required and double ropes will be useful on complex routes.

Hard Very Severe (HVS) These are advanced routes, demanding a determined approach coupled with cunning and experience. Double ropes, micro-wires and camming devices are generally required.

Extremely Severe (E1, 2, 3 etc.) This is the top grade, now split into several categories. Most enthusiasts will aspire to climb the famous E1, E2 and E3 routes, and in time will probably succeed. E4 and E5 routes are either exceptionally serious or technically very demanding. Routes graded E6 and upwards represent the most difficult and/or serious routes in the country.

The numerical grade indicates the maximum technical difficulty that will be encountered on the pitch. The system is unbounded, allowing for future increases in standard. At present it extends from 1 to 7. Each category is further subdivided by adding the letter a, b or c. Technical grades are not readily applied to the easier routes and so those in common use are: 4a, 4b, 4c, 5a, 5b, 5c, 6a, 6b, 6c, 7a, 7b, 7c. A complete beginner should be able to solve 4a moves, whereas relatively few climbers will ever develop the finger strength or technique to lead those rated 6c or harder.

The crux pitch of a typical *VS* climb would rate 4c; that of an *HVS*, 5a; and of an *E1*, 5b. Using those as the yardstick, an unusual combination of overall and technical grade will reveal something special about the climbing. For instance the crux moves on a route grad-

ed *VS 5a* will be very well protected, whereas those on an *E1 5a* will not be, the implication being that a *VS* leader will only attempt 5a moves in a safe situation, whereas an *Extreme* leader will expect to deal with moves of that difficulty regardless of the seriousness.

Aid Routes

Aid routes are given wholly numerical grades:

A0 Aid moves on mostly free routes.

A1 Straightforward aid climbing.

A2 Routes with some awkward reaches or suspect placements, or severely overhanging routes climbed on reliable *in situ* placements.

A3 Serious routes with several awkward placements or reaches on overhanging and/or suspect rock.

A4 Serious routes of all types, involving several marginal placements.

A5 Serious routes involving many marginal placements and with long fall potential.

INTERNATIONAL GRADING COMPARISONS

No direct comparison exists between systems, so the relationships implied here are very approximate. Only the most commonly compared grades are shown.

UK	UK (technical)	FRANCE	UIAA	USA
VS	4c	5a	V+	5.7
HVS	5a	5b	VI	5.8/5.9
E1	5b	5c/6a	VI+	5.10a/b
E2	5c	6b	VII	5.10c/d
E3	6a	6c	VIII−	5.11a/b
E4/5	6b	7a/b	VIII+	5.12a/b
E6/7	6c	7c/8a	IX+	5.13a/b
E8/9	7a	8b/c	X+	5.14a/b

Glossary

Not all terms listed here appear in the main text; they are included as an aid to deciphering guidebooks and magazine articles.

The glossary assumes an understanding of the following three common terms:

1. **Anchor** General term for a temporary or permanent fixing point for the rope.
2. **Crack** Any fissure in the rock varying in width from less than a millimetre to a few tens of centimetres.
3. **Hold** Any small rock feature used by the hands or feet for balance or support.

ABMG Association of British Mountain Guides (qualified professional instructors).

Abseil Descent achieved by sliding down a fixed rope.

Abseil sling/loop Short length of cord used to link abseil ropes to abseil anchor; prevents jamming during retrieval and avoids need to abandon a karabiner.

Accessory cord Low-stretch rope of between 4mm and 8mm diameter.

A cheval Means of crossing or ascending a knife-edged ridge or arete by straddling the feature as though it were a horse and then shuffling along.

Aid point Anchor (nut, peg, sling, etc.) to which a sling is attached for use as a makeshift hand or foothold.

Aid route Route climbed largely by pulling up on aid points instead of natural holds.

Alternate leads The even allocation of pitch leads by climbers of similar ability to avoid having to swap belay anchors after every pitch. Also called leading through.

Amphitheatre Large recess in the cliff face, tens or even hundreds of metres wide.

Angle peg V-shaped piton placed in wide cracks.

Arete Sharp-edged rock feature similar to the exterior corner of a building.

Artificial Refers to a route which seeks out difficulties despite the proximity of easier rock to which the climber could escape.

Artificial climbing Alternative term for aid climbing.

Ascender Mechanical device used as mobile hand grip when ascending a fixed rope.

Back and foot (backing up) Method of climbing a chimney by pressing the back and feet (or knees) against opposing walls and raising each alternately.

Back off Retreat intimidated from the prospect of making a difficult move.

Back rope Method of protecting the second from a pendulum fall on a traverse by allowing one rope to remain clipped to a runner at the start of the traverse.

Back-up Subsidiary anchor which is fixed as a failsafe in case the original either breaks or pulls out.

Balance climbing Method of climbing where most of the body weight is supported by footholds, the hands being used merely to maintain balance.

Bandoleer Shoulder sling used to carry equipment.

Belay anchor An anchor which secures the belaying climber.

Belay brake/plate/tube Friction device used when belaying the rope. Under load, the brake forces the rope around a sharp bend and thus eventually stops it sliding through. Also used as an abseil device.

Belaying Means of handling the rope (usually through a friction device) to safeguard a companion. The term is sometimes improperly used for belay anchor.

Big wall climbing Multi-pitch (often multi-day) ascents of vertical 1,000m+ cliffs using aid climbing techniques.

Biner American abbreviation of karabiner.

Bivouac (Bivi) To spend the night on a mountain, voluntarily or otherwise.

Blind move A move to gain a hidden hold.

Block Partially detached piece of rock usually a half metre or so high.

BMC British Mountaineering Council (governing body of the sport).

Body harness Elaborate harness which ensures that the body is maintained in an upright position after a fall.

Bold climbing Intimidating climbing, usually up vertical or overhanging rock, which responds best to a confident approach.

Bollard Squat, flat-topped rock pinnacle a metre or so high.

Bolt Metal anchor fixed into a hole previously drilled in blank rock. Consists of a threaded sleeve, a high-tensile bolt and a bolt hanger incorporating an eye through which a karabiner may be clipped.

Bolt route An aid route climbed using bolts as the main means of progress.

Bong V-shaped piton placed in cracks several centimetres wide.

Bouldering Unroped climbing on small outcrops.

Bowline Knot commonly used when tying on to the climbing rope.

Bridging (US – Stemming) Means of ascending V-shaped rock features by working the feet up opposing walls.

Bulge Small, rounded overhang or short section of overhanging rock which can usually be overcome in one reach.

Buttress Large, definable section of a cliff usually bounded by gullies or couloirs.

Cairn Small pile of stones erected to mark the start of a route, mountain summit, etc.

Camming device Anchor comprising sprung metal cams which expand automatically to fit any width of crack within its expansion range.

Capstone Slab of rock which blocks the exit from a chimney.

CC Climbers' Club (major national club with responsibility for producing guidebooks).

Chalk Light magnesium carbonate, in block or powder form, rubbed onto fingers for drying sweat and thereby improving grip on difficult moves (leaves unsightly white marks on the rock unless used in moderation). Carried in a chalk bag slung around waist or clipped to harness.

Cheating Ascending a free climb by unfair means, for example pulling up on runners.

Chest harness Chest support which when combined with a sit-harness produces a type of body harness.

Chickenhead Protruding and usually firm lump of rock used as a hold or to support a sling runner.

Chimney A vertical fissure into which most or all of the body will enter (willingly or otherwise).

Chimneying Method of ascending a chimney by wedging and raising the body using palms, back, knees, feet – anything.

Chock Alternative term for a nut.

Chockstone A rock found wedged in a crack. It may have arrived naturally or been placed there as a runner.

Chop route Poorly protected climb from which a fall may well prove fatal.

Classic abseil Basic method of abseiling which uses the rope alone to provide sitting support and frictional control of the descent.

Classic route Major route widely acclaimed for its quality.

Clean climbing Alternative term for free climbing.

Cleaning Removing lichen, grass, soil, loose rock, etc. from a potential new route prior to the attempt.

Climbing wall Training facility constructed, usually indoors, to resemble a rock face.

Clove hitch Knot sometimes used when securing to a belay anchor.

Col Prominent notch in a ridge or a saddle between neighbouring mountains.

Combined tactics A precarious means of overcoming a holdless section of a climb – usually immediately above a belay ledge – by standing on a companion's back or shoulder.

Committing move A move beyond which there is no hope of dignified retreat.

Corner Rock feature similar to the interior corner of a room.

Couloir A broad gully, tens of metres wide.

Cow's tail Short length of rope clipped between harness and aid point to support body weight.

Cruise Fluent ascent of a difficult route without recourse to yo-yos.

Crux The most difficult move, sequence or pitch of a climb.

Cwm (Corrie, Cirque) Valley or large hollow in the mountainside, usually hundreds of metres across.

Delicate move A precarious move using small holds.

Descender (Descendeur) Mechanical friction device used when abseiling.

Diedre (US – dihedral) French word widely used as an alternative term for a groove or corner.

Direct belay Time-saving method of belaying the rope using an Italian friction hitch.

Double fisherman's Knot used when joining two ropes.

Dynamic belay A belay method (principally the waist belay) which deliberately allows extra rope to slide through the hands while arresting a fall in the hope of easing the jolt on the falling climber or, more importantly, on marginal runners or belay anchors. Most belay methods are in fact dynamic to some degree.

Dyno An advanced move used in overcoming a blank section of rock. The climber springs up using the legs alone until it is possible to grasp a handhold. In extreme cases this becomes a leap.

EBs Trade name of the once ubiquitous rock boot.

Edging Technique of using small footholds by applying the inner edge of the boot sole. Also refers to rock boots particularly suited to this technique.

Escapable Section of climbing which is easily quitted for a less demanding alternative.

Etrier Short ladder made from nylon webbing and used as a foot support on aid routes.

Exposed move/pitch Section of climbing on which the climber becomes aware of the drop below and is likely to be intimidated by it.

Extension sling (Extender) Loop of rope or tape used to lengthen a runner.

Face climbing The mixture of balance climbing techniques, laying away and so on called upon when ascending a vertical or near-vertical open sweep of rock.

Fall factor An indication of the severity of a fall based on the peak force developed in the system (as opposed to the distance fallen).

F&RCC Fell and Rock Climbing Club (major national club with responsibility for producing guidebooks).

Figure-of-eight Knot with several applications. Also refers to a common type of descender.

Finger lock Twisting the fingers in a narrow crack to provide a firm support.

Fixed protection Runners left in place to make subsequent ascents faster or easier to complete.

Fixed rope Length of rope left permanently in place to make subsequent ascents faster or easier to complete.

Flake Rock feature measuring anything from 1cm to 1m across formed by partial peeling or eroding of the surface layer.

Flared crack Crack which widens near the surface and so offers only insecure jams or runner placements.

Free climbing Climbing a route without resorting to pulling up on runners and so on.

Friction climbing The technique of climbing near-holdless rock (usually slabs) largely by the support of sole friction alone.

Friend Trade name for the original self-expanding camming device.

Gardening Alternative term for cleaning.

Gear General term for climbing equipment. Also (loosely) an alternative term for protection.

Girdle traverse A route which crosses the cliff from one side to the other, usually at mid-height.

Glacis Slab angled at about 15–30 degrees.

Graded list List of routes from one region compiled, often controversially, in ascending order of difficulty.

Granite Type of compact and coarse-grained volcanic rock.

Greasy rock Rock made slippery by a coating of damp moss or lichen.

Gripped up Rendered immobile by difficult climbing and the fear of falling.

Gritstone A compact, coarse-grained and generally reliable rock type common in the Pennines and Peak District.

Groove Rock feature similar to a corner but generally more obtuse (shallow groove) or more acute (V-groove).

Gully A trough several metres wide, usually extending the full height of the cliff.

Half-rope Rope of around 9mm diameter. The term implies that it should only be used in conjunction with another half-rope.

Hand traverse Sideways movement along a flake or narrow ledge supported positively only by the hands.

Hanging stance A position where the belayer, in the absence of a ledge, is supported by the belay anchors alone.

Hawser-laid nylon Climbing rope, now obsolete, of the open (i.e. sheathless) type of construction.

Heel hook Gymnastic move in which the body is temporarily supported by placing the heel on a hold above the head.

Hexentric (Hex) Type of nut made from alloy bars of irregular hexagon cross section.

Incut Small, in-sloping finger hold.

Inescapable Section of climbing not easily quitted for less difficult climbing nearby.

In situ Refers to equipment (usually an anchor) left permanently in place.

Italian friction hitch Sliding knot used as an alternative to the belay brake.

Jamming Means of ascending cracks by wedging the fingers, hands or feet.

Jug Large, secure handhold (derives from the term jug handle.) Also to 'jug up' a fixed rope using ascenders.

Jumar Trade name for a once-common type of ascender, hence the phrase 'to jumar up' a fixed rope.

Karabiner Metal clip primarily used as an intermediate link between the climbing rope and a runner.

Kernmantel Nylon climbing rope of core-and-sheath construction.

Kletterschuhe Robust rock boots fitted with a stiff, treaded sole.

Knifeblade Type of thin bladed piton.

Knife edge An especially narrow ridge or arete.

Krab Common shortened version of the term karabiner.

Lasso Thankfully rare means of continuing a climb by throwing a loop of rope over a rock projection and swarming up it.

Layaway move A momentary layback applied with one hand and foot while reaching for a conventional hold.

Layback (US – lie back) Strenuous and often precarious means of ascending a corner crack or vertically aligned flake by leaning back and walking the feet up a holdless wall while gripping the edge of the crack or flake with the hands.

Leg loops Component of a sit-harness which supports the thighs.

Limestone Type of fine-grained sedimentary rock, usually vertical and frequently overhanging, commonly found in inland and coastal areas throughout Europe.

Live Rope That part of the rope between belayer and climber (as opposed to dead or slack rope which lies in reserve).

Locking karabiner Type of karabiner fitted with a sleeve to prevent accidental opening.

Lock off To hold fingers or elbows in a tightly bent position to reduce the strain on muscles when resting or placing protection on overhanging rock. Also to secure a belay or abseil device in order to free both hands for some other task.

Lower off Means of regaining the stance after a fall or failure by allowing the rope to support the climber's body weight while the belayer gradually pays out rope.

Mantelshelf (Mantel) Small ledge above holdless rock gained in the manner of a swimmer emerging from a pool (and often with equal inelegance).

Marginal placement A poor runner thought likely to fail if subjected to the force of even a short fall.

Micro-nut (Micro-wire) Small wired nut used for protecting the narrowest of cracks.

Moving together Time-saving method of partially protected climbing in which two roped climbers ascend simultaneously.

Niche A small, shallow cave perhaps only a metre across.

Nose Protruding mass of rock, from several to tens – even hundreds – of metres across.

Nut General term for the metal wedge type of anchor.

Nut key Strip of metal used to aid the removal of awkward nut placements.

Objective dangers Risks to climbers posed by stonefall, lightning and other natural phenomena.

Off-width A crack which is too wide to be climbed comfortably by conventional hand-jamming techniques.

On-sight lead A difficult route climbed without the benefit of prior knowledge gained during abseil inspection or a top-roped ascent.

Overhang Rock which bulges out beyond the vertical. Its underside may be horizontal like a ceiling but more often slopes up like the inside of a pitched roof.

Overlap Small overhang, usually less than a metre across.

Peg Common alternative term for a piton.

Peg hammer Tool used for inserting pitons into cracks.

Pendulum (Pendule) Method of swinging across on the rope to gain another line of ascent. Also refers to the type of fall which results from slipping from a traverse.

Pinch grip Type of protruding handhold utilised by gripping the rock between fingers and thumb.

Pinnacle Partially detached pillar of rock, usually several metres high.

Pitch Section of route between consecutive belay ledges.

Piton Metal anchor consisting of a blade (which enters the crack) and an eye (into which the karabiner is clipped).

Placement Alternative term for an anchor.

Pocket hold Surface flaw in the rock, usually caused by water erosion, which offers a secure hold.

Polished rock Holds worn smooth by regular use.

Positive hold A flat rather than sloping hold of any size from a few millimetres to a few centimetres.

Pressure hold A hold at around waist level, usually sloping, used typically when bridging to support the heel of the hand while the foot is raised.

Prodder Alternative term for a nut key.

Protection General term for the security offered by runners.

Prusiking Means of ascending a fixed rope using the support of loops held in place by prusik knots which slide upwards but lock in place when loaded.

Psyche up Prepare mentally for a difficult route (a climber is 'psyched out' when forced to abandon a climb through irrational fear).

Psychological runner A poor anchor placed mainly to boost confidence before attempting a difficult move. The climber pretends that the runner will hold a fall even though a clinical assessment suggests that it will fail.

Pumped Dramatic loss of strength, usually accompanied by pain, caused by overuse of muscles on a strenuous climb.

Quartz White, crystalline rock which commonly occurs in bands within other rock types.

Rack The selection of equipment (nuts etc.) carried up a climb.

Rack up Store protection equipment on the harness loops or bandoleer in a consistent order.

Ramp Narrow slab which slants diagonally across a rock face.

Rappel Alternative term for abseil.

Reverse Climb back down the move, sequence or pitch just ascended.

Rib A tall, slender protrusion of rock.

Ridge A raised crest of rock, perhaps extending the full height of the cliff.

Rock-over A dynamic means of attaining a standing position on a high foothold in the absence of handholds.

Roof Usual term for an overhang which has a horizontal underside like a ceiling. This may be anything from 1m to 20m across.

Rope drag The cumulative effect on the leader of the rope passing through runners and around rock edges.

Rope-length A pitch equivalent in distance to the full length of the rope.

Rope off Abandon a climb by abseiling down to the ground.

Runner An anchor placed in the hope of minimising the length of a fall.

Run-out The distance climbed above the belay or, more usually, above the last point of protection.

RURP Type of piton with a thumbnail-sized blade (derives from the term Realised Ultimate Reality Piton).

Sack hauling The technique, usually applied on mountaineering or big wall routes, of climbing a pitch unburdened then hauling up the rucksack afterwards.

Safety rope Secondary rope used to safeguard a climber when abseiling or prusiking.

Sandstone A fine-grained, compact, but sometimes unreliable rock type commonly found in Cheshire and south-east England.

Scoop A shallow depression in the rock face, usually a few metres across.

Scrambling Simple climbing on large holds.

Scree (US – talus) Unstable accumulations of stones found on or below cliffs.

Screwgate Alternative term for locking karabiner.

Second The climber who belays the leader's rope and then ascends with the protection of a rope held from above by the leader.

Serious climbing A move, pitch or route which is potentially dangerous, either because of loose rock or lack of protection.

Shake out A partial resting place on a strenuous pitch where the hands may be removed in turn and shaken to encourage blood flow and restore strength.

Shoulder belay Early method of belaying, now virtually obsolete.

Side-pull Vertically aligned handhold used to maintain balance.

Single-rope Rope of around 11mm diameter which is considered strong enough to be used in isolation.

Sit-harness Harness which supports waist and thighs and to which the climbing rope is attached.

Sit-sling Improvised sit harness.

Skyhook Metal hook placed over a tiny flake and used as an aid point for precarious support.

Slab Any expanse of rock approximately angled between 30 and 70 degrees.

Slings Loops of rope or tape, from 20cm to 2m in length, having several applications.

SMC Scottish Mountaineering Club (major national club with responsibility for producing guidebooks).

Smearing Technique of using small, sloping footholds by applying the sole of the boot. Also refers to rock boots particularly suited to this technique.

Snaplink Alternative term for karabiner.

Soloing Solitary climbing whether roped or unroped.

Spike A finger of rock used as a hold or anchor.

Stance A ledge part-way up the route where climbers regroup before attempting the next pitch.

Star rating Route quality indicated in guidebooks by the presence of one to three asterisks.

Static rope Low-stretch rope used for accessory cord and other subsidiary purposes but not as the main climbing rope.

Sticht plate Alternative term for a belay brake.

Sticky boots Rock boots soled with high-friction rubber.

Stitched sling Webbing or tape commercially sewn into a loop.

Stomach traverse An ungainly crawl along a ledge on which it is impossible to stand because of bulging rock above.

Tape Nylon webbing.

Tape knot Knot used when making loops from nylon webbing.

Technical climbing Sequence of climbing involving several puzzling moves.

Tension traverse Means of traversing across blank rock by using the rope tensioned through a nearby runner as partial support.

Terrace A flat area several or tens of metres wide and possibly extending the full width of the cliff.

Thin climbing Difficult climbing using small, infrequent holds.

Thread Anchor formed by feeding a sling through a natural rock tunnel or around a chockstone.

Through route Tunnel-like exit from a chimney.

Tie-off A short sling fixed around a partially inserted piton or camming device stem to reduce leverage.

Topo Stylised diagram of a route showing the location of belay ledges and main features.

Top roping Means of safeguarding an ascent by first walking round to the top of the route and throwing down a rope end.

Traverse Any part of a route, from a couple of metres to tens of metres, which involves climbing across instead of up.

Tyrolean traverse Spectacular but usually unnecessary method of crossing a ravine by sliding across a rope anchored to both sides.

UIAA Union Internationale des Associations d'Alpinisme (international governing body of mountaineering).

UIAGM Union Internationale des Associations des Guides de Montagne (international union of qualified professional guides).

Undercut Upside-down hold used to maintain balance.

Unprotected Section of climbing where runners are poor or absent.

Vegetation Assorted plant life obscuring rock holds.

Vibram sole Trade name for a common type of treaded boot sole.

Waist belay Method of belaying without using a belay brake.

Waist belt A simple harness or the waist component of a sit-harness.

Wall Rock face angled steeper than about 70 degrees.

Wedge Method of climbing off-width cracks using shoulder and leg jams. Also an alternative term for a wedge-shaped nut.

Well-protected Section of climbing where runners are reliable and frequent.

Wire Type of runner made from a nut threaded on a wire loop.

Yo-yoing Repeated attempts on a route where the leader is lowered down for a rest after each failure.

Useful Addresses

British Mountaineering Council (BMC)
177–179 Burton Road
West Didsbury
Manchester M20 2BB
(Tel: 0161 445 4747)

Courses, publications, access, insurance, etc.
This is the best single source of information
and addresses.

Cordee Books
3a De Montfort Street
Leicester LE1 7HD

Main distributors of UK and foreign maps,
guides, technical handbooks and narratives on
mountaineering subjects.

Glenmore Lodge
National Outdoor Training Centre
Aviemore
Inverness-shire PH22 1QU
(Tel: 01479 861276)

Plas y Brenin
National Centre For Mountain Activities
Capel Curig
Betws y Coed
Gwynedd LL24 0ET
(Tel: 01690 720280/366)

Bibliography

GUIDEBOOKS

Listed here are the club guides which give comprehensive information on some of the more popular British climbing venues, along with the selected route guides which are most useful when planning a visit to an unfamiliar region. These books are revised regularly and so titles may vary from year to year. Guides to less popular areas, and to climbs of mainly local interest, have not been included; these will be stocked as a matter of course by equipment suppliers in the areas concerned. Most major specialist retailers will stock a wide selection.

The following abbreviations have been used for guide publishers:

SMC: Scottish Mountaineering Club
F&RCC: Fell & Rock Climbing Club
YMC: Yorkshire Mountaineering Club
BMC: British Mountaineering Council
CC: Climbers' Club

Scotland

Comprehensive:
Glencoe and Glen Etive (SMC) Accessible climbing of all standards in Glencoe plus unique friction slabs in Glen Etive.
Ben Nevis (SMC) Classic 400m+ ridges plus hard routes on Carn Dearg.
Skye (SMC) Spectacular, medium-grade classics on rough gabbro.
Northern Highlands (2 vols) (SMC) Remote mountain crags in magnificent settings.
Cairngorms (SMC) Wide variety of climbing, much of it on remote mountain crags.

Arran, Arrochar and Southern Highlands (SMC) Island granite peaks plus accessible mountain crags and outcrops.

Selected:
Rock Climbing in Scotland (Constable)
100 Classic Climbs in Scotland (Central and Southern Highlands) (The Crowood Press)

Lake District

Comprehensive:
Langdale (F&RCC) Good climbing of all grades on Gimmer and Pavey Ark above a scenic valley.
Scafell and Eskdale (F&RCC) Long routes of all standards on excellent rock on the fells.
Borrowdale (F&RCC) Valley crag climbing in a delightful setting.
Dow, Duddon and Slate (F&RCC) Big routes of all grades on the perfect rock of Dow Crag.
Gable and Pillar (F&RCC) Mountain classics on the Napes and fabulous Pillar Rock.

Selected:
Rock Climbing in the Lake District (Constable)
100 Classic Climbs in the Lake District (The Crowood Press)

Northern England and Peak District

Comprehensive:
Yorkshire Limestone (YMC) Mid-grade outcrops plus the forbidding walls of Malham, Gordale and Kilnsey.

Yorkshire Gritstone (YMC) Uncompromising outcrop climbing at Almscliff and Brimham plus secluded venues for more private struggles.

Kinder and Bleaklow (BMC) Low and mid-grade grit routes in wild, remote moorland settings.

Froggatt (BMC) Popular grit climbs of all grades.

Stanage (BMC) Something for everyone on four miles of peerless Stanage grit.

Derwent Valley (BMC) Several fine outcrops including the low-grade slabby grit of Birchens.

Staffordshire Gritstone (BMC) Grit climbers' Valhalla at the Roaches and Hen Cloud.

Peak District Limestone (3 vols) (BMC) Mixture of peaceful riverbanks and thundering road sides, but the climbing is the thing: steep, white and frightening.

Selected:
On Peak Rock (BMC)
Rock Climbing in Northern England (Constable)
Rock Climbing in the Peak District (Constable)
100 Classic Climbs in Yorkshire and the Peak District (2 vols – Limestone, Gritstone) (The Crowood Press)

North Wales

Comprehensive:
Ogwen and Carneddau (CC) Many routes in the lower grades for early climbs and first leads, plus remote classics in the Carneddau.

Llanberis Pass (CC) Sombre valley with famous climbs in the middle and higher grades.

Clogwyn Du'r Arddu (CC) Awe-inspiring routes in the upper grades on one of Britain's major mountain crags.

Tremadog (CC) Sun-drenched outcrop climbing for experts at Tremadog; damper delights for beginners in the Moelwyns.

Gogarth (CC) Sea, sun, and frightening cliffs. Good climbs are HVS or harder.

Selected:
Rock Climbing in Snowdonia (Constable)
100 Classic Climbs in North Wales (The Crowood Press)

Southern England and Wales

Comprehensive:
Pembrokeshire (CC) Miles of vertical sea cliffs and lots of sun. Endless one pitch opportunities at HVS or harder.

Avon and Cheddar Intimidating climbing in limestone gorges near Bristol.

Chair Ladder and the South Coast (CC) Routes of all standards on Cornish granite; spiritual home of the sea-cliff climber.

Bosigran and the North Coast (CC) Tougher climbs on major Cornish sea-cliffs.

Southern Sandstone (CC) Small outcrops gaining stature by virtue of their isolation.

Selected:
South West Climbs (Cordee)

TECHNICAL BOOKS

The books listed here deal with peripheral aspects of the sport not covered in depth in the main text.

The Hillwalker's Handbook (Ashton, The Crowood Press) Describes the techniques of roped scrambling, mountain navigation, etc.

The Handbook of Climbing (Fyffe and Peter, Pelham) Includes sections on winter and Alpine climbing.

A Manual of Modern Rope Techniques (Shepherd, Constable) Includes improvised rescue techniques.

Mountain Navigation (Cliff, via Cordee Books) Concise paperback of essential map and compass techniques.

First Aid for Hill Walkers and Climbers (Renouf and Hulse, Cicerone) Convenient paperback manual giving realistic advice on recognising and treating injuries.

MAGAZINES

Climber All aspects of rock climbing and hill walking in Britain and continental Europe plus some international coverage.

High Similar to *Climber*. Official journal of the British Mountaineering Council.

On the Edge Mainly high-grade rock climbing in Britain and continental Europe plus some international coverage.

Index

HARMLESS WRONGDOING

Long Loan

This book is due for return on or before the last date shown below

The MORAL LIMITS

VOLUME FOUR

NEW YORK OXFORD

of the CRIMINAL LAW

Harmless
Wrongdoing

JOEL FEINBERG

OXFORD UNIVERSITY PRESS

Oxford University Press

Oxford New York Toronto
Delhi Bombay Calcutta Madras Karachi
Petaling Jaya Singapore Hong Kong Tokyo
Nairobi Dar es Salaam Cape Town
Melbourne Auckland

and associated companies in
Berlin Ibadan

Library of Congress Cataloging-in-Publication Data
(Revised for vol. 4)
Feinberg, Joel, 1926–
The moral limits of the criminal law.
Includes bibliographies and indexes.
Contents: v. 1. Harm to others—v. 2. Offense to others—
v. 3. Harm to self—v. 4. Harmless wrongdoing.
1. Criminal law—Philosophy. 2. Criminal law—Moral and ethical aspects.
3. Crimes without victims. I. Title.
K5018.F44 1984   83-13431
ISBN 0-19-504253-0
ISBN 0-19-506470-4 (PBK)

2 4 6 8 10 9 7 5 3 1

Printed in the United States of America